"Deprenyl has a great future i[...] Only now is its potential as a q[...] compound being recognized and documented by scientists throughout the world on various diseases of the nervous system. *(Editor's note: Alzheimer's disease, Parkinson's disease, Multiple Sclerosis, stroke, etc.)* Of great importance to researchers is the ability of L-deprenyl to rescue dying or injured nerve cells. *(See Abstract on page 259, Ed.)*

Because of L-deprenyl's promising beneficial effects in disease treatment and prevention, its nerve cell survival enhancing properties and reported negligible risk for developing side effects at low dosage, I can forsee extensive future use of L-deprenyl in disease prevention."

T. P. A. Kruck, Ph.D.
Director, National Brain Research
Foundation, Toronto, Canada

"Deprenyl protects the brain's 'engine of life' — the vital dopaminergic system."

Dr. Joseph Knoll
Chairman, Dept. of Pharmacology
Semmelweis University, Budapest, Hungary

"Deprenyl can be the single most important therapeutic element available to enhance well-being and the quality of life. Some experience quantum leaps to better life. Some just seem to age slower."

Dr. Ray C. Wunderlich, Jr.
St. Petersburg, FL 33701

"*Deprenyl* bears testimony to the arrogance of the FDA who withheld it from those in need for six long years. If Americans knew of the dozens of 'wonder' drugs used in Europe but denied to them by the FDA, they would demand the authority of the FDA be limited to the testing and rating of drugs for safety."

Dr. B. B. Lee
Chicago, IL 60606

"The discovery of deprenyl is to brain diseases and neurological disorders a medical breakthrough that ranks with the discovery of penicillin for bacteriological diseases — and more — because deprenyl also protects the brain from the ravages of aging diseases. Deprenyl is the first true anti-aging, life extension drug."

Dr. Ronald Klatz
President, American Longevity Research Institute
Chicago, IL 60614

"Deprenyl has been proven to have extraordinary therapeutic potential for Parkinson's disease with negligible side effects. In addition there is compelling evidence that this drug has neuroprotective and anti-aging properties, and may well be of help in Alzheimer's disease. Clearly the cellular mechanisms of action of L-deprenyl deserve further investigation."

Gwen Ivy, Ph.D.
Associate Professor of Anatomy
and Cell Biology and Psychology
University of Toronto

DEPRENYL

*is sold in the United States in
tablet form, under the trade name*

ELDEPRYL

(See Publisher's Note page 265)

DEPRENYL
THE ANTI-AGING DRUG

DISCLAIMER

At one time I wrote, "deprenyl is safer than aspirin" only to have Dr. Kruck admonish me saying, "aspirin is not safe; some people have allergic reactions." And, even though an allergy or serious side effect has yet to be reported from taking deprenyl -- it must be taken as medically prescribed. This book is not intended to provide medical advise. Charles Hallberg, publisher.

DEPRENYL
THE ANTI-AGING DRUG

ALASTAIR DOW

HALLBERG PUBLISHING CORPORATION
Nonfiction Book Publishers - ISBN 0-87319-036-X
Delavan, WI 53115 • Clearwater, FL 34618

ISBN Number 0-87319-036-X
Library of Congress Catalog Card Number 92-074929
Copyright © 1993 by Alastair Dow
All Rights Reserved
Printed in the USA. First printing May 1993.
Book designed and typeset by Xpress Graphix.
Portions of this book were taken from Dow's
prior book, The Deprenyl Story, published in
Canada in 1990. No part of this book may be repro-
duced without written permission of the publisher:

HALLBERG PUBLISHING CORPORATION
Phone: 1-800-633-7627

CONTENTS

FOREWORD

SINCE THE PUBLICATION in Canada (1990) of Alastair Dow's initial book on deprenyl (*The Deprenyl Story*) there have been many new studies that confirm and extend the evidence of deprenyl's remarkable life extension benefits.

This research indicates that deprenyl is probably even more effective in preventing Parkinson's disease than in treating it, and suggests several mechanisms of action by which deprenyl can rescue dying neurons (brain cells). New studies also confirm that deprenyl is definitely an effective treatment for Alzheimer's disease, and suggest that it may be able to prevent the disease as well.

In 1990, the primary evidence that deprenyl can slow aging came from Dr. Joseph Knoll's extraordinary finding that deprenyl can extend radically the maximum lifespan of laboratory rats. Since then, there have been several new studies showing that deprenyl can prolong the lifespan of different strains of rats, although the degree of lifespan extension in these studies has been more modest than in Dr. Knoll's study.

Furthermore, there is now evidence that deprenyl may be beneficial in the treatment of many other neurological conditions including multiple sclerosis, which has led a Canadian researcher to suggest that deprenyl provide a safe therapy for many types of neurological

1

damage, just as aspirin is an all-purpose therapy for pain and inflammation.

Deprenyl For Alzheimer's Disease

This year approximately 200,000 Americans will be diagnosed with Alzheimer's Disease. They will join the 4-5 million Americans already afflicted with this terrible disease. Alzheimer's patients (and their loved ones) must deal with the loss of the very essence of what it means to be a human being. They must face the progressive disintegration of their memory and personality until they cease to exist as individuals.

At diagnosis, Alzheimer's victims are invariably told by their physicians that there is no effective treatment for their condition, and that they are going to experience progressive deterioration of their mind and body until they die. The fact that almost everyone diagnosed with Alzheimer's disease is given such a fatalistic prognosis is cruel and unfortunate because of the growing evidence that deprenyl can provide substantial benefits for the victims of Alzheimer's disease, with little risk of adverse side effects.

The fact that deprenyl — which is an FDA-approved drug — is a safe and effective therapy for Alzheimer's disease is one of the best kept secrets in America. It is a secret because of the FDA's suppression of scientific information about the benefits of unapproved uses of approved drugs. The FDA not only forbids companies selling deprenyl to advertise about deprenyl's ability to help Alzheimer's patients, the agency also discourages journalists from writing about it as well. The result is that the overwhelming majority of physicians in this country simply don't know that deprenyl is a safe-and-effective treatment for Alzheimer's disease.

The reason being that deprenyl has only been approved by the FDA for the treatment of Parkinson's disease, not for Alzheimer's or for aging, or for low sex drive, or for any of the other uses for which there is scientific evidence of benefit in humans.

Benefits Of Deprenyl In Alzheimer's Patients

A daily dose of 10 mg. of deprenyl has been shown in controlled, double-blind studies to reverse many aspects of the progressive mental deterioration in mild-to-moderately impaired Alzheimer's patients, thereby improving the quality of life of these patients for up to six months. Among the mental functions that have improved in Alzheimer's patients receiving deprenyl are the ability to recall a series of words or numbers, to concentrate on matters of importance, to comprehend short stories, to copy drawings, and to remember events and concepts over extended periods of time. Alzheimer's patients receiving deprenyl become less irritable, less depressed, less anxious, and more relaxed than those receiving placebo. They are friendlier, more talkative, and more interested in participating in (and enjoying) a wide variety of social activities including housekeeping, shopping, building and repairing things, travelling, and going to parties.

Mechanism Of Action

The rationale for the use of deprenyl in Alzheimer's patients is the drug's profound effects on several brain chemicals called neurotransmitters that carry messages from one brain cell (neuron) to another. The neurotransmitter that appears to play the most important role in learning and memory is acetylcholine, which is one of the primary targets of the disease process in Alzheimer's patients. However, scientists have found that drugs which affect only the cholinergic system (which involves acetylcholine) are only slightly successful in treating Alzheimer's patients, and that other neurotransmitters play key roles in learning, memory, concentration, movement, coordination, and mood fluctuation — all of which are affected adversely in Alzheimer's disease.

Among the other brain neurotransmitters affected adversely in Alzheimer's disease are dopamine, norepinephrine, and phenylethylamine, all of which are oxidized (degraded) in the brain by the enzyme monoamine oxidase B (MAO-B). In the early 1970s, scientists found a progressive increase in brain MAO-B activity with advancing age in humans, which appears to be responsible for many of the physical and mental deficits of aging. They later discovered that brain levels of MAO-B in Alzheimer's patients are much higher than in normally aging persons, and that the exceptionally high levels of MAO-B in Alzheimer's patients produce excessive degradation of dopamine, norepinephrine, and phenylethylamine, which, in turn, leads to a serious decline in learning, memory, concentration, coordination, and sex drive in these patients.

Deprenyl is a selective inhibitor of MAO-B (at 10 mg. a day) which appears to improve the physical and mental condition of Alzheimer's patients by reducing (by up to 90%) the MAO-B-induced degradation of dopamine, norepinephrine, and phenylethylamine. Deprenyl may also improve the condition of Alzheimer's patients by interfering with the free-radical-mediated destruction of brain cells in these patients.

Studies In Alzheimer's Patients

The fact that deprenyl is a safe-and-effective treatment for Alzheimer's disease has been demonstrated in at least four controlled studies in humans in the United States and Italy. One of the earliest clinical studies of deprenyl in Alzheimer's patients was a double-blind, placebo-controlled trial conducted in the mid 1980s by scientists at the U.S. National Institute of Mental Health in Bethesda, Maryland and the University of Rochester School of Medicine in New York state. In this trial, which was conducted by Drs. Pierre N. Tariot, Trey Sunderland and Robert M. Cohen, 17 mildly-to-moderately-impaired Alzheimer's patients (5 males and 12 females) were given daily doses of placebo (for 7 days), 10 mg. of deprenyl (for 28 days), and 40 mg. of deprenyl (for 35 days). Thirteen of the patients were given a second course of placebo for 14 days after receiving deprenyl.

The scientists found that treatment with deprenyl resulted in significant improvements in behavior and cognitive function when the patients received 10 mg. per day of deprenyl, and lesser improvement (with greater side effects) when they received 40 mg. per day of deprenyl. Among the behavioral changes observed in patients receiving 10 mg. a day of deprenyl were decreases in anxiety, depression, physical tension, agitation, and psychotic episodes; and increases in verbal communication, participation in social activities, and positive feelings about life. Among the cognitive benefits of treatment with 10 mg. of deprenyl were improved concentration, learning, and memory . . . especially on complex learning tasks requiring sustained attention.

In a more recent clinical trial conducted by neurologists Luigi Piccinin, Giancario Finali, and Massimo Piccirilli at Perugia University in Italy, 20 Alzheimer's patients with mild-to-moderate impairment were given 10 mg. of deprenyl and placebo in crossover fashion during two 3-month periods. The Italian scientists found that deprenyl produced statistically significant improvements in word fluency, digit span recollection, long-term spatial memory, the ability to copy drawings, and verbal memory and concentration. Another important finding of the study was that deprenyl treatment improved the patients' motivation to get things done, to do well on complex tasks, and to enjoy their lives.

The largest clinical trial of deprenyl in Alzheimer's disease to date was conducted in 112 patients by Drs. A. Mangoni, M.P. Grassi, L. Frattola, and associates at several neurology clinics associated with the University of Milan in Italy. Patients with slight, moderate, or moderately severe mental deterioration were randomly assigned to two groups, with one group (65 patients) receiving 10 mg. a day of deprenyl, and the other group (47 patients) receiving a placebo over a three month period.

The patients receiving deprenyl showed significant improvement on tests which assessed primary, semantic, and episodic memory. They also showed improvements in performing the daily activities of living as well as in their enjoyment of life. The authors of the study concluded that: "In view of the positive cognitive and behavioral results achieved and of the large numbers of patients who did not manifest the expected further deterioration in daily activities, deprenyl seems to be an effective treatment for patients with Alzheimer's disease."

When scientists at the University of Southern California in Los Angeles gave 14 patients 10 mg. of deprenyl daily for four weeks, they found overall improvements in agitation, mood, and word recall. They also found that several patients in the study, who had previously been treated with THA (tacrine), showed improvement on both regimens, which led them to suggest that a combination of THA and deprenyl might work better than either drug alone. The rationale behind this suggestion is that THA, which inhibits the enzyme (acetylcholinesterase) that degrades acetylcholine, works by an entirely different mechanism than deprenyl. There have been anecdotal reports that the combination of deprenyl and THA (plus lecithin) may be an especially effective therapy for Alzheimer's disease.

The Safety Of Deprenyl

A consistent finding in the clinical studies of deprenyl in Alzheimer's patients is the lack of adverse side effects. In the University of Milan study, for example, only 3 patients originally enrolled in the study (4.4%) dropped out because of problems associated with deprenyl. In none of these cases were the side effects severe enough to cause harm to the affected patients. The most common side effects reported, after taking 10 mg. of deprenyl on a daily basis, have been dizziness and orthostatic hypotension. These side effects (and others) have been slight and easily reversible. The vast majority of Alzheimer's patients who take deprenyl tolerate it extremely well, with no undesirable side effects.

Another consistent finding in these studies is that, although the beneficial effects of deprenyl for learning, memory, and behavior are relatively small, the degree of improvement in these patients tends to increase with time. Since the longest period that patients have been followed in these studies has been six months, it's quite possible that patients receiving deprenyl would continue to experience even greater degrees of improvement after taking the drug for longer periods of time. It also is important to note that the patients receiving placebo in these studies continued to deteriorate in function during the course of the study, which parallels the fate of all untreated Alzheimer's patients. As a result, even the small improvements in function in Alzheimer's patients taking deprenyl are highly beneficial for patients who would otherwise be deteriorating.

Deprenyl And Chelation

The latest news on treatment of Alzheimer's patients comes from scientists at the University of Toronto, who have been treating patients with intramuscular injections to chelate aluminum and iron, removing these toxic metals from neurons in the brain. (Iron has been shown to generate damaging free radical reactions and autopsied brains of Alzheimer's victims contain higher-than-normal amounts of aluminum.)

According to University of Toronto researchers, the aluminum/iron chelation treatment reduced the rate of deterioration in quality of life skills by fifty percent (50%) with additional benefits achieved by co-treatment with deprenyl.

Alzheimer's Patients Should be Taking Deprenyl

Although more research is needed to explore the effects of deprenyl (by iself or combined with other drugs) in Alzheimer's disease, there are several good reasons why Alzheimer's patients (and persons at risk for the disease) should be taking deprenyl right now.

1. The findings of at least four controlled clinical trials have shown that the daily intake of 10 mg. of deprenyl by Alzheimer's patients significantly improved attention, concentration, learning, memory, the ability to perform the daily activities of life, and the quality of life in most of the patients tested.

2. The safety of taking 10 mg. per day of deprenyl has been demonstrated not only in controlled clinical trials with Alzheimer's patients, but also in thousands of patients with Parkinson's disease, some of whom have been taking the drug at this dosage level on a daily basis for many years.

3. By taking deprenyl, Alzheimer's patients are likely to benefit from the anti-Parkinson's disease and anti-aging effects of treatment with deprenyl in addition to its ability to counteract the lethal effects of Alzheimer's disease.

While deprenyl alone is not a cure for Alzheimer's disease, it clearly improves the quality of life of Alzheimer's patients and may slow the progression of the disease. The fact that millions of Americans afflicted with Alzheimer's disease (and their physicians) are unaware that deprenyl is a safe-and-effective treatment for Alzheimer's disease is a national tragedy. Hopefully, this book will be the first step in a nationwide campaign to inform Americans about the benefits of deprenyl as a treatment for Alzheimer's and other neurological diseases.

Rescuing Neurons In The Brain

Recent studies at the University of Toronto suggest that deprenyl may have the ability to prevent the death of the dopamine-producing neurons in the substantia nigra region of the brain which are lost in Parkinson's disease. Drs. W. G. Tatton and C. E. Greenwood have shown that injections of deprenyl into mice can rescue neurons dying from exposure to a highly toxic metabolite of MPTP, a chemical which induces Parkinsonism in both animals and humans.

When mice were pre-treated with MPTP for five days, analysis of their brain tissue showed that an average of 37-42% of dopamine-producing neurons were lost gradually over a 20-day period. When they were treated with deprenyl after being exposed to MPTP, they lost only 14-16% of these neurons. When dying neurons were treated with deprenyl in tissue culture, the scientists were able to recover, for the first time in medical history, up to 70% of the dying neurons.

A recent report from scientists in Parma, Italy demonstrated that treating aging (19-month-old) rats with deprenyl until 24 months of age protected the neurons in the hippocampus region of the brains of these rats from aging-related damage. (The hippocampus is one of the primary areas of the brain in which memories are stored). The scientists found that deprenyl treatment significantly reduced the age-dependent accumulation of lipofuscin (aging pigment) and the age-related impairment of mossy fibres in hippocampal brain cells.

These findings suggest that deprenyl may prevent the loss of neurons associated with the onset of Parkinson's disease and Alzheimer's disease, both of which are caused by the accelerated loss of neurons, which also are lost during normal aging. Some scientists now believe that we would all come down with Alzheimer's and Parkinson's disease if we lived long enough. The ability of deprenyl to rescue dying neurons suggests that deprenyl may slow down the rate of aging in the brain, which may correspond to its ability to extend mean and maximum lifespan in rats.

Deprenyl Boosts Antioxidant Enzyme Activity

Another recent finding which suggests that deprenyl may be able to protect against the loss of neurons that underlies both Parkinson's disease and the aging process as a whole, is that deprenyl produces significant increases within the brain of the antioxidant enzymes superoxide dismutase (SOD) and catalase (CAT). A joint study by scientists at the Tokyo Metropolitan Institute of Gerontology in Japan and the University of Toronto demonstrated that the administration of deprenyl to young male rats for several weeks caused a major increase in SOD and CAT in certain brain regions such as the substantia nigra, but not in the hippocampus or cerebellum region of the brain. This finding suggests that deprenyl may bolster the brain's intrinsic capacity to ward off the toxic effects of excessive free radical activity, which may be involved in aspects of aging.

Extending Lifespan

Perhaps the most beneficial effect of deprenyl is its apparent ability to slow down the course of normal aging, which is the underlying cause of the lethal diseases of aging and the defining factor in determining maximum lifespan in humans (100 plus years). The deleterious effects of aging lead inevitably to death by robbing us of the health and vigor that keeps us alive and disease-free and enables us to enjoy our lives. If deprenyl is a true anti-aging therapy, as the evidence suggests it is, its clinical benefits will be greater than any other therapy in history. It will not only help us to prevent lethal diseases, but could enable us to live longer, healthier, and more youthful lives well beyond the century mark.

The remarkable results of a lifespan experiment by Dr. Joseph Knoll at the Semmelweis University of Medicine in Budapest, Hungary were initially reported in *The Deprenyl Story.* Dr. Knoll found that injection deprenyl (0.25 mg./kg.) into albino rats three times a week, starting at the advanced age of two years (which is equivalent to about age 65 in humans), could restore youthful sexual activity in these animals and could, amazingly, enable them to live far longer than control animals. The longest-lived rat in Dr. Knoll's control group survived for 164 weeks whereas the shortest-lived rat in the deprenyl group lived 171 weeks, with the longest-living rat in the deprenyl group surviving for 226 weeks.

These unprecedented findings, in which the maximum lifespan of aging animals was extended radically, suggest that chronic deprenyl treatment in humans might enable us to live in good health for 130 years or more, even if the treatment was started late in life. Since then there have been several studies confirming that deprenyl can extend lifespan in laboratory rats. In one of these studies, scientists at the University of Toronto give male Fischer rats injections of either deprenyl (0.25 mg./kg.) or saline every other day, starting at 23-to-25 months of age. The deprenyl-treated animals showed a significant increase in both mean and maximal lifespan. The increase in mean lifespan, however, was only 16%, considerably less than in Dr.

Knoll's experiment with Albino rats. However, the differences in lifespan were largest in the longest surviving animals, suggesting that earlier onset of treatment might have been more beneficial for the animals.

In a more recent study at the Tokyo Metropolitan Institute of Gerontology, 35 male Fischer rats were given injections of smaller amounts of deprenyl (0.5 mg./kg. three times a week), starting earlier in life (18 months of age), with 35 control animals receiving injections of saline. The Japanese scientists found a 15% increase in the life expectancy of deprenyl-treated rats from 18 months of age, and an increase in life expectancy of 34% in the deprenyl-treated rats after 24 months of age.

Although the results of these studies are highly promising, it should be noted that in all three studies, deprenyl was given by injection rather than by oral administration, and that no study has yet been published showing an increase in lifespan in animals given the drug orally. Since deprenyl is commonly given orally in humans (in the form of pills or liquid), we look forward to the results of lifespan studies in which deprenyl has been administered orally. However, the clear-cut benefits of oral deprenyl treatment in patients with Parkinson's and Alzheimer's disease, and its demonstrated ability to inhibit the aging-related increase of MAO-B, and to increase the body's own antioxidant enzymes (SOD and CAT), is strong evidence that oral treatment with deprenyl may be effective in slowing the underlying loss of brain cells that occurs in normal aging, as well as in a wide variety of neurologic diseases.

One thing we do know, deprenyl is the first true anti-aging drug whose wonders continue to unfold as scientists probe its multifaceted activity.

SAUL KENT
President
Life Extension Foundation
Hollywood, FL 33022-9120

PREFACE

WHEN I FIRST HEARD about deprenyl in the summer of 1987, I knew it only as the name of a drug that had helped a close friend to overcome the debilitating symptoms of Parkinson's disease. It is difficult for a healthy person to be empathic with someone whose life seems no longer worth living, though perhaps less so through knowing someone who has been reprieved. It was by watching the repair of my friend's body and the rebirth of his spirit that I became interested in deprenyl. How could a drug, a chemical compound, alter the behavior of the mind and the performance of the body in the most profound way?

In researching this book I learned that the word *drug* has different shades of meaning. Increasingly, in common usage, it has come to mean a substance whose use is forbidden by law, such as heroin or cocaine, or a substance whose use may be legal but that has addictive and perhaps other undesirable side effects — drugs such as nicotine and alcohol.

In its broader, "ethical" context drug is a word whose definition has had to be altered during the past 50 years. Until the mid-1950s it was sufficient to say that a drug was "a chemical used in the diagnosis, prevention, treatment, or cure of disease." With the introduction of the oral contraceptive in 1955, diseases were no longer the only targets of ethical drugs. The new and more general definition became "any chemical agent that affects living processes."

Deprenyl drew my attention to the world of drugs for a number of reasons. It was suggested that deprenyl was a miracle drug that might help us live longer, better lives. I wondered how. Deprenyl had been used for some years by tens of thousands of people in countries in Europe and elsewhere in the world, and yet it was not available in North America. I wondered why. There were also claims, which seemed fanciful, that deprenyl not only improved the quality of life, but also had the potential to extend the maximum human life span. The latter claim seemed to be venturing into the world of science fiction because, while the average person has progressively lived to be older, the maximum human life span has not altered in thousands of years.

Given the choice, not many people would choose to live beyond 100. The prospect of simply running out the clock, of waiting for Father Time to strike midnight, of being a burden to family and others, is hardly enticing. But what intrigued me was the evidence that deprenyl might make people want to live longer because it would help them to remain active and "youthful" in their later years. They could expect to continue to have hearty appetites and to continue to indulge in the pleasures that most of us believe will be lost to us when we grow old. Deprenyl would help people overcome what is the single greatest fear among those of us who are past the adolescent stage — the fear of the physical and mental deterioration that accompany old age and senility.

The evidence in favor of these claims made on behalf of deprenyl was, at first, difficult to sort out. The drug worked wonders on rats: in clinical tests they were alert and frisky well into what was previously thought to be their old age, and they lived longer than ever thought possible. Rodents are not Homo Sapiens, but when a drug has certain effects on rats, it is at least suggestive that it will have similar consequences for humans.

On humans the effects of a drug are often more difficult to measure. Humans are more complicated than other animals, and they live in surroundings that are rendered "unnatural" by complex societal and pervasive environmental influences. There are also, in humans, practical as well as ethical obstacles in the measurement of a drug's effects on the brain, or mind.

For years it was accepted, in Europe at least, that deprenyl gave relief from symptoms of Parkinson's disease by reducing the required dosages of levodopa, which is the standard therapy for Parkinson's, and therefore minimizing the discomfiting side effects of levodopa as well as prolonging its efficacy. Pilot studies, in North America as well as in Europe, showed that deprenyl had therapeutic effects in people suffering from other chronic diseases associated with aging. For example, deprenyl has been shown to subdue the antisocial tendencies of people suffering from the form of senile dementia known as Alzheimer's.

Deprenyl was finally approved by the U.S. Food and Drug Administration in July 1989, and then only for use in what are called the middle and late stages of Parkinson's disease. But the drug's coming-of-age in North America was heralded in the last months of 1989 when researchers found that deprenyl not only relieved the symptoms of Parkinson's disease, but almost certainly slowed its progress. *This was the first time any drug had been shown to delay the symptoms of a neurological disease.*

With this finding deprenyl became the first of a class of new drugs aimed at halting the degeneration of brain cells. If the brain conducts the orchestra of life, does it follow that deprenyl and its descendants will extend life and, more importantly, improve the quality of life?

This book was written because of a number of curiosities.

Starting from the beginning, how are drugs developed? How do chemists build or modify the molecular structure that gives a drug its particular properties? How do scientists build a drug (which is, in fact, a molecular compound) so that it has the desired effect on "living processes"? How is the efficacy of a drug measured? By what kind of human and mechanical process is it determined that a drug deserves to be presented for scrutiny, given the stamp of approval, manufactured, authorized for sale and, ultimately, prescribed for use? Are drugs — or rather the business of drugs — truly international, or are there barriers to their free migration?

In another category of curiosities: who are the people who touch upon this entire process?

The pharmaceutical business, even though it is concerned with, and to some extent responsible for, the maintenance and/or repair of health, is in many respects like any other business. Success requires a recognition that the product — in this case, a drug — has value. The product, therefore, must be promoted before it can become known and available for use. And, in order to be brought to market, even a drug with known therapeutic qualities must meet the test of commerciality.

Economic criteria dictate every step of the process, from the synthesis of a molecular compound by a chemist, its study by a pharmacologist, its testing by a clinician, its approval by regulatory bodies, and its eventual dispensing by a pharmacist. Maximization of return on capital investment is the ultimate goal of every successful business.

Scientists are fond of saying that the perceptions of any object are highly subjective and even that the very fact of observation can alter the structure and/or behavior of the object. What I found, in the case of deprenyl, was that for a long time the perception of the drug and its merits also depended on whether the observer was located inside or outside North America.

There is one last comment that speaks to my own initial ignorance of the subject of drugs. A few short months ago I did not realize the extent to which a drug may affect different people in different ways — and sometimes not at all. This is among the reasons that deprenyl has been the subject of such controversy. In the case of people with Parkinson's disease, deprenyl's obvious effects differ according to the stage of the disease at which the drug is administered.

It is relatively easy to prove a drug helps someone who is sick, which is why deprenyl was finally approved by the FDA for use in mid-to-late stages of Parkinson's disease. It is hard to prove a given drug, or nutrient, can prevent a disease even if all evidence and logic so indicates. However, as doctors throughout the world prescribe deprenyl as a life extension drug — a drug that protects the substantia nigra area of the brain and the dopaminergic system, thereby allowing mankind to live longer, healthier lives — deprenyl will be known as the miracle drug of the 21st century.

I am indebted to Morton Shulman, an indomitable man, for his encouragement in writing this book. Without Dr. Shulman I might never have had the opportunity to know Joseph Knoll or Donald Buyske, both of whom, like Shulman, are among the most interesting people one would ever hope to meet.

ALASTAIR DOW
Toronto, Canada

DEPRENYL
THE ANTI-AGING DRUG

1

THE MURAL AT
MADISON AIRPORT

✳ THE WAY HIS DOCTOR DESCRIBED IT, Gibson
Byrd could barely move. His body was stiff
except for a persistent trembling in his
limbs. His speech had a lazy slur, and he wore a blank
look on a face that had once been animated. Byrd had
spent his adult life as a teacher and artist in Madison,
Wisconsin; at the age of 62 both of those pursuits
seemed lost to him. His sense of self-worth was over-
taken by despair and depression.

It was the summer of 1986, eight years after Byrd
discovered he was a member of that legion of hundreds of thousands of North Americans caught in the
inexorable progression of Parkinson's disease. "PD"
has two primary consequences. It is a disease that
affects motor functions — its sufferers have increasing
difficulty transforming thought into action. In PD it is
not the flesh that is weak; it is the spirit that fails to
move it. The second consequence, perhaps even more
debilitating, is the knowledge that old age has arrived

prematurely. People do not die from PD; they just die sooner from some compounding ailment. In the meantime, as the symptoms of the disease become more pervasive, the window closes on that preciously short period of each day when even the routine tasks of living can be performed.

By the time a diagnosis of Parkinson's disease can be made, the disease is incurable. Medicine can only slow its progress and offer relief from its symptoms.[1] Byrd was fortunate, if it could be called good fortune, that by the time he was diagnosed as having PD in 1978, relief was at hand in the form a drug called levodopa. It used to be that there were only two treatments for PD. One was surgery, a hazardous adventure since the locus of PD is an abnormality, or "lesion," in the brain. The other form of treatment was drugs, all kinds of drugs, but mainly belladonna alkaloids, whose efficacy had little rational basis. They were empirical drugs: if they made you feel better, if they seemed to give some respite from the symptoms of PD, that was good. These drugs were not necessarily aimed at the site of the disease — a pea-sized portion of the brain called the substantia nigra — because the abnormality in that region of the brain was not understood until the late 1950s. Empirical drugs are judged by their end re-sult — "take an aspirin and you'll feel better" — and not because, by design, they repair some known bio-logical damage. Levodopa, in contrast, was a rational treatment: it was developed specifically to redress the chemical imbalance that originated in the substantia nigra and which had become recognized as the culprit in PD.

---

[1]Deprenyl is the only drug known to slow the progress of Parkinson's disease.

When levodopa arrived in the early 1960s, the very first rational drug treatment for PD, it was called, with justification, a wonder drug. Levodopa is not a cure for PD, nor does it slow the progress of the disease. But, for most people, it does relieve the symptoms of what is an entirely symptomatic disease. For two or three years, and perhaps as long as five or six years, levodopa holds at bay the symptoms of PD. Those are years of usefulness added to each life. After that, levodopa turns on its patients, its power diminishes, and its gathering of side effects becomes similar to, and sometimes worse than, the symptoms of PD.

By the grace of levodopa, Gibson Byrd had enjoyed benefits of those added years of productive life. Now, in 1986, all the symptoms of PD and all of the side effects of levodopa converged upon him. His akinesia, his loss of control over movement, was almost complete. He was, in the parlance of Parkinson's disease, "frozen."

Byrd was a transplanted Oklahoman who had spent 30 years teaching art at the University of Wisconsin. His own paintings had chronicled his life, drawing on his childhood in the Southwest, his service as an air force gunner during the Second World War, his involvement in the civil rights movement of the 1960s and, finally, the peaceful years in the countryside near Madison. Byrd was respected as a teacher. As a painter, he was regarded as a hobbyist.

So, in the summer of 1986, it seemed perverse to him when he was offered a commission to paint a mural for the new airport being built for Madison, the state capitol of Wisconsin. This would be an opus that would be seen by more people than any other he had done. In his community it would always be known as the "Gibson

25

Byrd mural." But the canvas was to be ten feet square, and the painting of it called for a tenacity and stamina that only an able-bodied man could summon. Byrd was hardly able-bodied. At best, he could function for only an hour or two a day, and even during those brief interludes he could never be sure when the symptoms of his disease would suddenly and unexpectedly recur. As it was, he had difficulty getting through each day — getting dressed, rising from a chair, navigating from room to room.

What is it like to be old? At that moment Gibson Byrd knew. His wife, Bonita, had been aware there was something wrong since 1978 when Byrd began to feel that first slight trembling in his left leg. Inwardly he was healthy. No stethoscope, no urinalysis, no blood tests could uncover a single thing wrong with Byrd. But as time went by, first the tremor, then the failure of his muscles to move his limbs the way they used to, his lack of balance, the excessive saliva in his mouth, showed that he had Parkinson's disease. Byrd came to the realization that many of the incapacities of old age would arrive before their time.

Parkinson's is a neurological disease — a disease of the nervous system. It most frequently occurs in its idiopathic form, meaning that the cause is unknown. It is insidious: it creeps up imperceptibly on its victims. And it is progressive, in that it gets worse with time.

The central nervous system — that is, the brain and spinal cord — defines what we are. It is the source and the reason for our total behavior, and it is also the means for us to change our behavior. Neurological disease may affect any of the things we are or do or feel — our movements, sensations memory, language, needs, desires, intellect — in short, all of our being.

When Gibson Byrd was diagnosed as a "parkinsonian" in 1978, he knew that an important part of his being was in a state of premature erosion. If we had been able to look inside his brain at the first signs of his infirmity, we would have seen an abnormal loss of black pigment in that tiny section of the midbrain called the substantia nigra. This would have indicated the premature death or deterioration of the nerve cells, or neurons, that produce a chemical substance called dopamine.

Dopamine cells occur in various organs and tissues of the body, but they are highly concentrated in the area of the substantia nigra, part of the brain's gray matter which plays an important part in the performance of our muscles and limbs. As the dopaminergic cells wear out and cease to produce dopamine, normal bodily movement falters. The brain and the body give way to the main defining features of PD — the tremor, rigidity of the limbs, and impairment of the voluntary control of movement. There is no pain, little loss of sensation or awareness, and the mental state, at first, usually remains well preserved.

This is what happened to Gibson Byrd at the early age of 54. He began to lose the freedom to determine his own behavior. He would not die from Parkinson's, but his life expectancy was shortened because he would die earlier from some other cause. Perhaps worse, there would be little quality of life during the time remaining to him.

Eight years later, in 1986, he was still alive, but he could not — or thought he could not — paint the mural he so much wanted to paint at Madison's new airport.

No country in the world is more rigorous than the United States in the screening, testing, and approval of

27

new drugs. Under the U.S. Food, Drug, and Cosmetics Act no drug may be marketed until it has been shown to be safe *and* effective.

Safety and effectiveness are measured on a relative scale, sometimes called a therapeutic index. If a drug were developed to cure a cancer, for example, the ruling Food and Drug Administration might approve the drug even if it had a relatively high degree of toxicity. Conversely an application to market yet another analgesic would have shown very low toxicity levels. It is a trade-off which currently is decided at the discretion of the FDA and not the marketplace, not the people in need.

To accumulate evidence upon which to decide whether a new drug is safe and/or efficacious when used in humans begins with an application to the Food and Drug Administration for an Investigational New Drug (IND) exemption, which allows the testing of a manufacturer's promising new drug on consenting humans.

No matter how much a new drug may be tested, in laboratories and on animals, the effects on humans cannot be accurately predicted. There has to be a person, or group of persons, to be the first to take the risk. The U.S. government safeguards the IND procedure, as much as it can, by requiring that subject patients be protected from "unreasonable and unnecessary risk" and that the testing be conducted only by medical experts qualified by training and experience to conduct clinical investigations.

Paul Nausieda is such a qualified person. He is an effervescent doctor whose early training, while he was at the University of Chicago in the early 1970s, was in the chemistry of sleep-wake disorders. During his time as a hospital resident, something happened that gave his career a new direction.

I had the opportunity to admit a middle-aged Italian real estate owner from the south side of Chicago. After we had admitted this man, we did an extensive neurological evaluation and could find nothing wrong with him (at least as far as the test data would show). He complained that he just couldn't do anything the way he had previously and was moving slowly. It was obvious that something was wrong with him, but we didn't seem to be able to make a diagnosis.

The attending physician was not very experienced and she also didn't know what to make of the clinical picture.

After a month in the hospital, a senior attending physician took over the floor. I presented the case to him as a neurological enigma.

We walked into the room and he said, "Good morning," to the patient and shook his hand. Without any further examination, he walked out of the room and said, "This man has paralysis agitans in its akinetic form."

It immediately became obvious to me that this was the correct diagnosis, though I hadn't considered it because the man did not have tremor. I think that it was probably the most humiliating moment in my residency, since I had always considered myself a fairly sharp diagnostician.

Shortly after this incident, Nausieda contacted Harold Klawans, a doctor whose name is famous in the treatment of Parkinson's disease, and asked if he could spend some time with Klawans's patients. People with Parkinson's, he learned, were unusual patients. Many who appeared to be doing well would insist they were deteriorating rapidly.

Nausieda became particularly interested in the interaction between the psyche and the soma (the whole organism), and in 1982 he began a series of teaching programs for Parkinson's patients identical to those programs previously offered only to physicians. He became involved in patient advocacy and left academic medicine to establish his own private clinical research facility.

Since then, when he is not ministering to patients at the Parkinson's Disease Treatment Center in Milwaukee, he has been on the road giving inspirational talks to groups of patients and their families. "It is my ego," he says. "I like to give people hope."

Nausieda was ever on the alert for ways to give hope to victims of Parkinson's disease. But where could hope lie? The prevention of Parkinson's depended on the discovery of its cause, and that cause — whatever it might be — seemed as elusive as ever. Finding a cure was unlikely because the seeds of the disease are planted many years before the emergence of its symptoms permits a diagnosis. That left only the possibility of finding a treatment that would halt or even slow the progress of the disease after it had been diagnosed.

In 1986 Nausieda applied to the Food and Drug Administration for an IND exemption that would allow him to make experimental use of a drug called deprenyl in patients with Parkinson's disease.

Deprenyl had been prescribed in Austria and Hungary since 1978 and in Great Britain since 1982, where it was used in combination with levodopa. It seemed to enhance the action of levodopa and, most important for those people in the latter stages of the disease, it often prolonged the duration of benefit of levodopa.

How deprenyl worked in the brain — the drug's "mechanism of action" — was not clear, however.

Nausieda had monitored the reports from Europe. He was aware that some Americans were going to unusual lengths to acquire the drug. Some were traveling to Europe to obtain it; in Southern California Parkinson's disease support groups were importing contraband supplies, at whatever prices were necessary, via Mexico due to the FDA's control of medicine in the United States.

He knew, further, that major U.S. pharmaceutical companies had been offered the rights to deprenyl, but had said no. These rights now resided with Somerset Pharmaceuticals, Inc., a small, struggling company that had somehow acquired access to drug technology from Hungary. Somerset was on the brink of bankruptcy, and the fate of deprenyl's approval by the FDA was very much in question.

The only FDA approved way to use deprenyl in the United States was on a limited experimental basis. Nausieda administered deprenyl to the first of his patients in the summer of 1986. Among them was Gibson Byrd, the artist from nearby Madison. After two weeks Byrd was able to reduce his daily dosage of levodopa.

31

His symptoms were mitigated, he recovered some of his energy, his daily "on" periods — during which he could control his movements — lasted much longer. Byrd was encouraged by his wife and by Nausieda to attempt to paint the mural at Madison airport. He finished the job two months later.

When Byrd began taking deprenyl it was, to him, a small white tablet made of compressed powders and incised with the letters *JU*. It was, simply, a pill he was instructed to take twice a day, once in the morning, and once before dinner. When Byrd's energy began to return, and as he spent long hours working on his mural, he wondered how this small pill could have so profoundly affected his life. He mused about the pill's active ingredient, *selegiline*, traveling through the body that was so recently inert, transported by his bloodstream, crossing the blood-brain barrier, and then somehow working to adjust the chemistry of his brain.

Byrd knew little about the origins of deprenyl. He knew that the drug had come form Hungary and that it had been used in Europe for many years. And he had heard the stories about deprenyl — the stories about its mystical, if not magical, powers.

Deprenyl was supposedly a drug that kept people young.

There was that system in the brain — the dopaminergic system — that regulated inner drives, that kept people young beyond their years. Deprenyl was a drug that kept people vibrant during the postdevelopmental stage, postponing the rust of old age. Animals other than humans tend to lie down and expire soon after they lose the power to procreate. What was it that sustained humans? No one had disproved the Darwinian theory of prolongation of the species, but what was the source of human motivation that continued long after menopause and, in the case of men, the climacteric? Was it somewhere in the brain, the central processor of all life's activity? Was it the dopaminergic system?

These were the fanciful notions that preoccupied Byrd as he painted his mural. Philosophically they were a far reach from Parkinson's disease, one of the apocalyptic disorders of the central nervous system that now engages so much of medical science's attention. But Parkinson's disease is a sensory disorder as well as a movement disorder. It also happens to be an age-related disease. If deprenyl had helped to relieve the symptoms of PD, had it not also issued a more general reprieve? The drug had certainly improved the quality of Byrd's life. Had it not also given him the promise of a longer life?

The evidence of the drug's usefulness in the treatment of Parkinson's disease was clinically proven. The evidence that deprenyl extended life span was also proven — but only in that favorite of laboratory animals, the rat. Here was abounding evidence that deprenyl reawakened sexual interest, but this type of evidence was largely anecdotal; it was not the kind of evidence that scientists, with their "due process" and "peer review," were prepared to embrace.

On one score there were no dissenters. Deprenyl, when used properly, has no harmful side effects. This quality is most important in any drug, and in hundreds of thousands of patient-years of experience in Europe there had not been one report of serious consequences from side effects.

Why then, Byrd wondered, had deprenyl taken so long to reach the shores of North America?

The truth about deprenyl was that it had been born in

Budapest in 1961 during a research program aimed at finding a new treatment for high blood pressure and/or depression. It was all but ignored until 1964 when a Hungarian professor of pharmacology, Joseph Knoll, thought he detected in the compound a property that prompted him to call it a "new psychic energizer," a term that had been coined only a few years earlier to describe a new class of antidepressant drugs. Deprenyl , Knoll believed, had that characteristic and, as well, possessed a mysterious "psychostimulant" effect similar to that caused by amphetamine. He suggested that the drug be tested in psychiatry "as a central nervous excitant drug of a new type."

There are hundreds of thousands of chemical substances with unexploited biological value. These substances, or molecules or compounds, never become known unless and until someone recognizes their potential value.

In the case of deprenyl Joseph Knoll was the person who recognized the peculiar properties of deprenyl and encouraged other scientists to investigate its potential. Knoll "developed" the drug. At the same time, deprenyl would have languished in obscurity had it not been "discovered" many years later by Dr. Walter Birkmayer, a Viennese doctor whose eccentricities include his willingness to try just about any drug to treat any disease.

Birkmayer opened the door to the worldwide use of deprenyl in the treatment of Parkinson's disease. However, the drug might never have come to North America had it not been for the patience and occasional stubbornness of Donald A. Buyske, a biochemist with the instincts of a research scientist and businessman, a rare combination. Buyske spent years introducing doctors to the drug, sponsoring tests to prove its safety and efficacy, raising the money to keep Somerset Pharmaceuticals alive, and cajoling the FDA to grant approval for its use. For his efforts he won the endless gratitude of people throughout the United States — such as Robert Tesher, a dentist in Plantation, Florida.

Tesher's wife, Leonora, noticed the first early symptom of Parkinson's disease when she was in her mid-forties. It was a trembling in her left arm, but while she could feel it, she couldn't see it. It didn't show. This phantom-like feeling was the beginning of a long ordeal for the Tesher family. For years doctors failed to diagnose Parkinson's. The more she complained, the more doctors became exasperated with her. "You're just a spoiled housewife," one doctor exclaimed. Leonora, who is a very nice woman, remembers this period well: "It was driving me nuts," she says.

Eventually Dr. Tesher sent his wife to the Mayo Clinic in Rochester, Minnesota, where a neurologist watched her walk into his office. Right away the doctor said, "You've got Parkinson's disease!"

Leonora began taking levodopa therapy, but she was one of those people who are especially susceptible to the drug's side effects. For one thing, she had this burning pain in her abdomen. Worst of all, there was the depression. Dr. Tesher took his wife to three different mental institutions. "She was one of those people," he says, "who just couldn't handle levodopa. It reached the point where she needed a nurse around the clock. She was a nonfunctioning human being. I couldn't leave her by herself for a moment."

In the spring of 1989 Tesher heard about deprenyl, but he couldn't find a doctor willing to prescribe it. In desperation he circumvented the FDA and imported the drug from outside the United States. By the third week after Leonora began taking deprenyl, "It was as though someone turned on a light switch. It was like somebody waved a magic wand. She was a new person. I got her back."

When the new Leonora attended her first meeting of a Parkinson's awareness group, the other members huddled around her. "Tell us about deprenyl," they said.

2

DANCING IN THE SANATORIUM

WHEN WE DECIDE TO TAKE A STEP — say with our right foot — the process is as follows: an impulse originating in the left hemisphere of the brain travels to the lower right limb, where the muscles used to put our foot forward contract and opposing muscles relax. At the same time, the muscles elsewhere in our body are prompted to behave in a way that accommodates the shift in balance. This entire process is physical and chemical. It is the result of an electrical stimulation being transmitted, by chemical means, between and among our nervous circuits.

It is not only the way we move. It is also the means by which we think and the way we feel. Theologians and philosophers may recoil at the thought, but modern science has relegated the mind — whatever "the mind" may be — to a metaphysical abstract. If there is such a thing as the mind, then the brain is its organ, and the brain is composed of cells, whose behavior is explained in terms of molecules, which in turn may be explained in terms of their atomic structure and the way they interact.

To a neurologist, nothing we do or think or feel cannot be explained by those physical and chemical changes within our bodies.

The father of molecular biology is generally conceded to be an Austrian physicist named Erwin Schrödinger. During 1943 and 1944, Schrödinger gave a series of lectures at Trinity College in Dublin, Ireland. In his halting English he made the provocative suggestion that physicists should begin to look at living organisms in the same way as they had always studied the composition of inanimate objects. It was Schrödinger's thesis that, as complex as the cells of the human body may be, they nevertheless bear certain resemblances to the cells of, say, a wooden table.

Schrödinger called all of these cells crystals. The cells that composed the wooden table were fascinating enough, he admitted, but the discipline of physics was making no contribution to an understanding of life. In contrast, chemists were making great advances in understanding the structure and behavior of living cells. These living, organic "crystals" were all the more fascinating and, while unpredictable compared to those of dead or inanimate objects, deserved the scrutiny of physicists as well as chemists.

Schrödinger used the following analogy to compare the two types of crystals:

> The difference in structure is of the same kind as that between an ordinary wallpaper in which the same pattern is repeated again and again in a reg-

ular periodicity, and a masterpiece of embroidery, say a Raphael tapestry, which shows no dull repetition, but an elaborate, coherent design traced by the great master.

Ever since the beginnings of modern medicine in the nineteenth century scientists had focused their attention on the chemistry of organ systems. But chemistry alone could never account for the behavior of humans or other animals. It was time to probe inside those organs — to study more than just the cells that compose them, but also the structure and activity and dynamic interplay among the molecules that make up those cells.[1]

Atoms and even molecules are far too small to be visible to the naked eye, and in Schödinger's day there were no microscopic devices that could begin to reveal the internal structures of living cells and the interaction of the molecules within those cells. It was to be another decade until the development of powerful new magnifying machines allowed scientists to account for the behavior of the body's organs at a molecular level.

With the help of new magnifying and imaging technology scientists learned about the basic mechanisms of the body's organ systems, and how these systems

---

[1] Schrödinger's lectures were collected in a small book entitled *What is Life?* (1944: Cambridge University Press). In it he concedes that it is impossible to have a unified and all-embracing understanding of how the human body works, but: "I can see no other escape . . . than that some of us should venture to embark on a synthesis of facts and theories, albeit with secondhand and incomplete knowledge of some of them — and at the risk of making fools of ourselves." Science still works that way. As the story of this book illustrates, success in science still comes from a combination of facts and theories, sometimes guided by instinct, and occasionally blessed by luck.

were sometimes disturbed or diseased. With advances in computer technology they could contemplate the synthesis of an infinite number of new molecular structures which, used as drugs, could bring about the chemical changes necessary to rectify any physiological damage. Instead of making drugs that might affect the whole animal, or even one organ, they were able to engineer drugs so that they had the desired chemical effect only at their site of action.

Drugs, therefore, became more specific. Although no amount of pharmaceutical innovation could produce a magic bullet — a drug that traveled directly to the site of disease and did only what it was supposed to do — drugs could be made that had fewer side effects. Side effects were always the major problem: one could never predict all the consequences of a new drug until it had been used in many thousands of patients. Human genetics, different stages of a disease process, and concomitant illness are compound variables that make predictions of side effects an exercise in statistics or at best an educated guess.

The understanding of the anatomical structure and function of the brain — its physiology — was enhanced in 1951 following the unusual behavior of a group of tuberculosis patients in a U.S. veterans hospital. The prognosis for tubercular victims was grim (because of their melancholic disposition as well as their terminal disease, patients were often called "crocks" by their doctors). The standard treatment for tuberculosis was streptomycin, an antibiotic first isolated in 1944 from the gizzards of chickens and later from soil samples. Although streptomycin helped to manage the disease, it caused patients to lose their sense of balance, and among its other side effects were impaired hearing sometimes leading to total deafness. Confronted with these side effects, doctors went in search of a more sympathetic treatment. They settled on a drug called iproniazid, a close chemical relative of another drug, isoniazid, which had been used in tuberculosis wards. The effects of iproniazid were startling and were later described in unusually blunt terms at an international symposium of scientists:

> Iproniazid was being used successfully in the treatment of tuberculosis in the fifties, but it had one serious disadvantage. In some patients it produced an undesirable behavioral activation. One of the early papers reporting the use of this substance in the treatment of tuberculosis in a sanatorium described the patients "dancing in the halls" — and it wasn't because they had seen their X-ray pictures. It was soon realized that iproniazid was a nervous system activator of some kind.

This bizarre episode came to the attention of other doctors in the United States who were treating hypertensive patients with a drug called reserpine. Recently reserpine had been isolated from Rauwolfia serpentina, a plant used as a sedative in India for 300 years. Reserpine was considered to be a valuable drug, but its continued use sometimes induced severe depression. It was decided to experiment with iproniazid concurrently with reserpine. One account of the result said: "Much to their delight, physicians were amazed to observe that after the administration of iproniazid,

41

patients — even terminal patients — were extremely cheerful and were highly optimistic about the future."[2]

It may seem a paradox now, but it was because of the apparent stimulative effect on the central nervous system, and the unknown psychological implications of this unseemly behavior, that iproniazid was withdrawn from use in 1952. Only in 1955 was it recognized as a new kind of drug, and it was called a MAO inhibitor because it worked by arresting the action of an enzyme called monoamine oxidase.

Within a year the apparent mood-elevating properties of MAO inhibitors were put to use in the treatment of depression. Several pharmaceutical companies designed their own MAO inhibitors, and their number proliferated. They became very, very popular.

Physicians now had, for the first time, drugs to treat serious incapacitating depressions that previously could be treated only by such radical procedures as lobotomy, electric shock, and insulin shock. The introduction of MAO inhibitors helped to depopulate mental institutions throughout the United States and elsewhere in the world.

Almost all drugs that affect the brain do so by their influence on synaptic transmission, which is to say, by affecting the chemical connections that bridge the natural gaps between and among the brain's nerve cells or neurons. It is difficult to picture this in the mind's eye,

---

[2]The story of iproniazid has been told many times in scientific and popular literature. The failure to exploit the drug for its behavioral side effects, instead of for its intended use as a tuberculosis treatment, drew the following comment in 1976 from Seymour Kety, the head of psychiatry at Harvard Medical School: "I think it provides a salutary description of how scientific discoveries are made and how one moves from the accumulation of fundamental knowledge to knowledge of immediate social value. It may also have a sobering effect on tendencies to target research."

but the brain, which is about the size of a grapefruit, is composed almost entirely of billions of neurons. While it was long thought that these neurons formed a network of connections, it is now understood that none of them actually "touches" another. The gaps that separate them are called synapses, and it is across these synapses that neurons communicate with one another. The medium of communication is a group of chemicals called neurotransmitters.

Until only a few years ago it was believed that communication among neurons followed the pattern of a chain reaction: one neuron sent an impulse to an immediate neighbor, which passed the message on to an adjacent neuron, and so on. Now it is believed that each of the billions of neurons may form simultaneous connections with up to 10,000 of its fellows. The brain, therefore, is not so much a continuous, complete circuit, it is a switchable network of neurons.

The easy analogy to describe the brain is that of a central processing unit. But that is misleading: information processing systems are built in a particular way and for a particular purpose, which we understand. We do not understand how the brain works because we did not build it to some particular design.

We have learned a great deal about the anatomy of the brain. We know much less about the brain's function, except that there is a close relationship between structure (anatomy) and function. We also know that the physiological workings of the brain's structure are carried out by neurotransmitters.

Among these neurotransmitters is a specific chemical substance called dopamine. It is the lack of dopamine — or at least the premature degradation of dopamine — that results in the symptoms we describe as Parkinson's disease.

Dopamine is a "biogenic" amine. It is an essential chemical that occurs in many parts of the body. But its highest concentration is in the region of the brain called the basal ganglia, a mass of gray matter in the basement of the brain that is important in the programming of bodily movement.

The basal ganglia includes a striped organ called the corpus striatum and another "nucleus" called the substantia nigra. The cells of the substantia nigra — called dopaminergic cells — produce dopamine, and — neuron to neuron — dopamine works its way throughout the motor pathways of the brain. One of these pathways, leading to the corpus striatum, is thought to be particularly vulnerable to the damage that leads to Parkinson's disease.

Dopamine acts as a messenger. If we were to isolate two dopaminergic neurons, the first would communicate with the second by emitting dopamine to build a humoral bridge to the second. Some of the dopamine thus released would be absorbed by the receiving neuron; some would be lost during the journey (a result of metabolism); and some would be recovered by the sending neuron. The last process of recovery is called "re-uptake." Dopamine, like all neurotransmitters, is constantly being synthesized in the brain, used to transmit messages across the gaps between and among neurons, and then inactivated by a chemical change. This system of synthesis, use, and inactivation is necessary to maintain just the correct amount of dopamine in the right balance with other chemicals. Too much dopamine, or too little, and the brain cannot function optimally. However dopamine is absorbed, metabolized, or excreted, it is essential to the continued efficiency of the body. It is a life-giving or biogenic chemical.

One of the characteristic changes in the body as we age is that the volume of essential chemicals is reduced. Dopamine degrades more quickly than most. Dopaminergic cells — concentrated in the region of the substantia nigra — are the fastest aging cells in the body. As dopaminergic cells decay, control over movement is diminished.

MAO inhibitors became more widely used in the late 1950s, and their mechanism of action became better understood. Like other enzymes, MAO is a protein that catalyzes and regulates the chemical reaction necessary for the efficient functioning of most of the body's cells. Enzymes control almost all of the biochemical reactions in our bodies. They are essential to all intermediary metabolism, whether the buildup (anabolism) of body constituents or their breakdown (catabolism). We could not live without them. Enzymes regulate chemicals that are naturally in the body, and when we ingest food or other chemicals, enzymes help to separate the parts we need to keep from the parts we need to waste. They are responsible for the production of all the organic materials present in living cells; they provide the mechanisms for energy production and utilization in muscles and the nervous system; and they fine-tune the intracellular environment.

So, to impede the work of enzymes is not something to be taken lightly. There is, however, a rationale for inhibiting the action of enzymes. On occasion, they overreact and oxidize or otherwise inactivate the substances whose presence they are supposed to modulate. The probability of this happening increases with age.

Of all the thousands of enzymes in the body, monoamine oxidase is the most ubiquitous and the one that has most captured the curiosity and fascination of scientists. MAO is everywhere in the body — in the liver, the stomach, the intestines, and other organs. In 1973 it was discovered that MAO also occurred in the brain.

In the liver one of the functions of MAO is to inactivate a substance called tyramine and to transform it into a harmless acetic acid. Otherwise, the tyramine might find its way unchecked into the bloodstream where it is capable of causing a dangerous increase in blood pressure.

In the brain, and especially in the brains of older people, MAO occasionally overreacts. Sometimes it destroys chemical neurotransmitters before they have lived out their usefulness. With the progression of age, an enzyme such as MAO is not necessary in such quantities to balance the chemistry of the brain.

The first MAO inhibitor, iproniazid, showed that it was possible to restrain monoamine oxidase when necessary. Against the depradations of MAO, iproniazid helped to maintain the stores of neurotransmitters in the brain. By that means, iproniazid helped to guard against depression. Another MAO inhibitor, developed some years later, took particular aim at the type of MAO that destroyed the neurotransmitter called dopamine. It was to be called deprenyl.

3

JOSEPH KNOLL
IN BUDAPEST

FROM A HIGH EMBANKMENT in front of the king's palace, the colored fountains of Margaret Island are to the left, the floodlit parliament buildings lie directly across the river, and in the distance, far beyond the baroque buildings of the old city, the oblong silhouette marks the research tower of Semmelweis University of Medicine, the tallest building in Budapest.

Professor Joseph Knoll (pronounced with a hard *k*) is the consummate guide. He is standing near the site of the original castle built by King Bela IV after the retreat of the Mongols in 1242. The palace was one of the important cultural centers of Europe until the Turks began to occupy most of the countryside surrounding this strategic bottleneck of the Danube. In the nineteenth century, when the Hapsburgs chose to reside in Vienna, Hungary became a nation unto itself, its people of obscure origin, not Slavic but surrounded by Slavic countries, with their own impenetrable Magyar language. Hungarians are different.

Knoll is an engaging man of average height whose appearance and demeanor belie his distinguished record as a scientist. He dresses conservatively, and well. His hair is wavy in the European manner, short, and mostly gray. Although stocky, he gives the impression of someone who looks after himself. Knoll is one of those persons whose age is difficult to guess. In the spring of 1989 he was approaching 64.

For someone who was born in Hungary and who has spent his life there, Knoll's English is fluent and, moreover, sprinkled with clever metaphors. His culture extends beyond his facility with language. He is actively interested in Impressionist and Modern art and he is quite at home comparing the melodic vitality of Bela Bartok with the symphonic poems of Franz Liszt. Whatever the conversation, it is suffused with Knoll's energy. Even seated he is kinetic. He is a good listener, but he would prefer to talk. He is a man who lives as though every moment were at a premium. Joseph Knoll has verve.

Knoll's air-conditioned Audi stands out from among the congestion of Russian-built Ladas as he pulls up to the city's oldest restaurant, Regi Orszaghas. He is greeted with familiarity, just as he draws recognition elsewhere in this city of two million anonymous faces. Although much of his life is spent in the cloister of laboratories, Knoll is a personage. He wears his status comfortably.

On the way back through Pest on the other side of the river, Knoll drives through the Square of Heroes where a statue of Joseph Stalin stood until after the uprising of 1956. "'Power tends to corrupt,'" he says, quoting Lord Acton. "'And absolute power corrupts absolutely.' I read that in a book written in 1920 by Arnold Toynbee."

Knoll reads and learns and works. That is his "drive" — a word he uses frequently and which is at the basis of his work as a scientist. "Work is the really human activity. Science and art," he says. "The striving for collecting money is a sham activity." His own existence is guided by respect for human life and purposeful endeavor. In Knoll's mind the two go together. "The most precious thing in the world is a child, and the most important thing is to help the child to find purpose and satisfaction — and that will come from work."

Knoll has many of the traits of a teacher, which he continues to be as chairman of the department of pharmacology at Semmelweis University of Medicine. He has that effervescent enthusiasm for his subject that is common to people who are so effective at imparting knowledge. He is restless and animated. His voice rises, and sometimes, for emphasis, descends to a whisper. He frequently resorts to pen and paper to illustrate his points.

In the laboratory, where Knoll is most at home, he peers at a short piece of artery taken from a rabbit's ear and suspended in aqueous solution. "So you stimulate the nerve terminal, and it is innervated and it secretes a chemical, and the chemical goes to the smooth muscle, and the smooth muscle contracts and the blood pressure is increased. And you measure, and you measure, and you measure — again and again and again.

"We are trying to find a substance that will inhibit the secretion of that chemical and therefore reduce the blood pressure. The problem is that there are many millions of substances, and always we are looking for just the right one."

Deprenyl became the right one. That Knoll and others happened upon it was a result of chance, instinct, and experience — the combination that leads to so many fortuitous discoveries, and which in science is called serendipity.

All of today's technology has done little to alter the random nature of the search for new drugs. The exactness of statistics cannot be applied to chemistry or, for that matter, physics. In the search for pharmaceuticals the scientific method prevails — study the phenomena, dream up a hypothetical explanation, and devise experiments to see if the hypothesis is reflected in nature. And even if the hypothesis turns out not to be valid, you have learned something. "I am almost as happy when an experiment doesn't work," Knoll says. "It means I have reduced my level of ignorance."

Pharmacology is the study of drugs and their effects on the body, but it would be a mistake to assume that Knoll, a pharmacologist, developed deprenyl as part of a quest to find a treatment for Parkinson's disease. Knoll, who is far from being without conceit, would argue that he has an even higher calling than finding a treatment for a disease. He would say that he uses drugs in order to understand the physiology of the organism. When a drug interacts with a body's cells, what does the result tell us about the body's physiology — its physical and chemical makeup and its function? If we can understand how the body's systems work, does it not then follow that we will learn the reasons these systems sometimes malfunction and so be able to devise a cure? "Nature makes the rules," Knoll says. "The effects of drugs help us to understand those rules. When we understand the physiology, we can protect it from disease."

To Knoll, deprenyl was a tool that he thought might help him to understand the dynamic processes of the brain. He used it to test various hypotheses, first on rats and other animals and then on humans, hoping that it would reveal something — anything — about the physiology of the brain. The live brain — the functioning brain — does not submit to easy examination.

STRUCTURE OF A MIRACLE

S E L E G I L I N E (deprenyl)

Only subjective feelings, and the effects of drugs, help to explain its mysteries.

Knoll kept deprenyl alive for 15 years after the drug was born as a test molecule in a laboratory in Budapest in 1961. He saw in the molecular compound certain properties that he found appealing — not because of the drug's potential in the treatment of a particular disease, but because it had a mode of action that he thought "peculiar" and that helped him to understand, by inference, how the brain worked. He persisted in exploring the action of the drug through all those years, even though it was ignored or dismissed by doctors and scientists around the world.

Only in 1977 was it discovered that deprenyl could improve the lot of those who were afflicted with Parkinson's disease. When a doctor in Vienna, Walter Birkmayer, announced that the drug "resulted in a statistically significant reduction in patients' functional disability," deprenyl found a compelling medical utility. Birkmayer's findings could find no better platform than *The Lancet*, the British medical journal. Knoll, who was barely known to Birkmayer, received no credit for the development of deprenyl.

Within a year the drug was on sale in Hungary, and by 1982, when it became available as Eldepryl in the United Kingdom, deprenyl had been prescribed to tens of thousands of people throughout Europe. In Parkinson's disease there is an international grapevine. The drug with the trade name Eldepryl became known in North America because a woman in Birmingham said she could now go shopping without fear of being frozen in her tracks, and because the plumber in Miskolc said he need no longer fear being arrested for clinging to a lamppost, wrongly accused of being inebriated. Drugs become famous because of stories like that. Like any other drug, deprenyl did not work for everyone, but to someone with Parkinson's disease that hardly mattered. It offered hope, and help to the vast majority.

As word of deprenyl spread to North America, there was a clamor for the drug, but another seven years would pass before deprenyl became available in the United States, due to FDA control of medicine.

Many drugs are "discovered" as a result of the astute observations of clinicians, and this was true in the case of deprenyl. It was Birkmayer, a clinician, who opened the door to the worldwide use of the drug. But it was Knoll who had nursed deprenyl from its conception; had contributed to the design of the original molecule; had participated in the testing of the drug, first in the laboratory and then on humans; and had demonstrated that the drug was free of harmful side effects. There were many other people involved, but Knoll had orchestrated this work over a period of many years. Although he was incontestably the father of deprenyl, he remained all but unknown outside the European scientific community.

Knoll is far from shy, but he would rather talk about his work than about his life. Like all prominent scientists, he carries a curriculum vitae at the ready. His, other than giving the year of his birth, 1925, is devoid of personal details. The professional background is impressive, as is his record of publishing: by 1989 he had written 77 scientific papers, co-authored 56, and played a lesser role in the preparation of another 113. Most were written in Hungarian or German.

Except for the broad outlines of his career, though, large gaps remained in the life of Joseph Knoll. A graduate of Budapest University Medical School in 1951, he became a physician who never practiced medicine. Instead, he chose to work in the department of pharmacology.

The father of pharmacology in Hungary was Ignaz Philipp Semmelweis, the famous obstetrician who in the last century observed that puerperal fever was transmitted among pregnant women by doctors who failed to clean their hands thoroughly. Semmelweis

was one of the persons responsible for modern steril-
ization procedures in the operating room. Because he
saved the lives of so many pregnant women, he was
acclaimed in Hungary as "the savior of mothers."
Knoll himself has written a historical monograph
about the history of pharmacology in Hungary. His
version fails to note, unlike so many others, that
Semmelweis was persecuted not only because he
accused the proud medical establishment of causing
needless deaths from infections, but also because he
was a Jew.

The accomplishments of Semmelweis led to the establishment of the first independent department of
pharmacology in Hungary in 1872. Since then there
have been only four chairmen of the department. The
third was Knoll's teacher, Bela Issektuz. The fourth
was, and is, Knoll.

On the fourth floor of the tower of Semmelweis
University, Knoll's name is prominently displayed as
chairman of the department of pharmacology. Two
secretaries act as sentinels outside his office in an an-
teroom whose walls are adorned by photographs of his
three predecessors. Inside Knoll's office, in front of his
desk, is a coffee table surrounded by a deep, leather-
covered couch and armchairs. His private bathroom is
en suite.

"Issekutz was a fine man and a good pharmacologist," Knoll remembers, "but he didn't speak foreign
languages. He spoke German. He was very much a
member of the German school of pharmacology. By the
time I took the chair in 1962, pharmacology had become an Anglo-American science. I changed the
language of the department to Anglo-American."

Issekutz cast a wide spell. In the years immediately following World War II, many young medical students at the University of Budapest chose to work in the department of pharmacology. Under Issekutz's tutelage, they concentrated on structure-activity relationships, which showed how the physical structure of drug molecules and the manner in which they interconnect with the body's cells combine to affect a drug's potency and selectivity. Selectivity is the most important quality of a drug. The more selectively a drug attacks targeted cells, leaving other cells relatively undisturbed, the freer it is from side effects.

Many of these students were to become professors of pharmacology, physiology, biochemistry, and the other emergent life sciences. Several became leaders of research laboratories around the world. Knoll was one of the few who did not leave his homeland.

From the beginning of his career Knoll was attracted to psychopharmacology — the study of the effects of drugs on the brain. Psychopharmacology was in its infancy, a new science that incorporated chemistry, neurology, psychiatry, and sociology — and sometimes even law and philosophy. The discovery, in the early 1950s, of drugs that affect behavior without altering consciousness revolutionized the practice of psychiatry: pills, as well as couches and institutions, became therapeutic options for people with mind disorders. With that development, there were all kinds of new questions, many of them ethical. Was it appropriate to tamper medically with the brain? How would the unknown effects of new brain drugs be tested? In human tests was a person with a psychiatric disturbance capable of giving consent for such tests? Who would be responsible for the consequences?

The brain was now being studied as a functioning organism and not as part of "the mind." Whereas behavior had long been the preserve of theology, and later philosophy and psychology, now behavior, including mood, thought, and perception, was regarded as the consequence of molecular changes in the brain.

Almost from the dawn of psychology the behavior of animals has been explained by the terms *association* or *connectionism*. Association refers to the mental linking or connection of objects or events and is said to account for the nature of our behavior. Accordingly, through learned associations, our nerves are stimulated in such a way that we respond in a certain manner.

In 1903 Ivan Petrovich Pavolv carried this concept much farther when he described a more complex set of responses. Pavlov was not a psychologist, but a physiologist, and he attempted to explain what had been called association by describing it as a conditioned reflex that occurs with and because of the formation of a temporary connection in the brain.

Knoll believed that Pavlovian theory failed to account for natural instinctive activity. He felt that certain kinds of behavior were the consequence not of known, external stimuli, but of stimulation from within the brain itself. The reflexes described by Pavlov were *conditioned*. Knoll postulated a theory that "drive-motivated behavior" was an *unconditioned* reflex associated with certain physic activities inside the brain.

The word "drive," in different languages, has subtly different meanings. In all of them, however, it refers to the fundamental instinct to satisfy our primeval desires. In every language and in every culture these are the desires whose diminution is associated with aging.

There is no universally accepted concept of drive, although it had long been agreed that each person's drives were aimed at satisfying their own particular purposes. Knoll, as had other scientists and philosophers, questioned this idea of purposive behavior. It did not explain to him the connection between subjective ideas and the physical mechanisms in the brain that determine how we perceive, think about, and act upon the environment.

Physiology so far had not explained everything about the workings of the brain. There remained a large gap between physiology and psychology.

In 1969 Knoll collected his thoughts in what became a book, entitled *The Theory of Active Reflexes: An Analysis of Some Fundamental Mechanisms of Higher Nervous Activity.* In it he set forth his explanation of "instinctive" activity as opposed to the Pavlovian reflex activity. Using rats, he demonstrated that the basic reflexes, such as the alimentary function (the desire for nourishment), have their origins in a specific activation of the central nervous system. He showed that an alimentary focus in the brain is activated not only by external stimuli, such as the sight of food or the association of a ringing bell with the imminent arrival of food, but because the need for food is signaled by certain deficiency-sensitive receptors in the brain.

The desire to *do* something, such as eating, arises from excitation. The desire *not to do* something arises from inhibition. The cause of inhibition, one of the least understood functions of the higher nervous system, is interrelated and inseperable from that of excitation. In his book Knoll showed that inhibition, like excitation, was also governed by what he called active reflexes. This was true of the drive to sustain the body through nourishment, the drive for sex, and the drive for survival. They were subjective, and not the result of some objective external stimuli.

If Knoll's theory was correct, then somewhere in the brain there might be an "active focus" that is the source of basic drives. Knoll came to believe that the active focus was the dopaminergic system — a broad term that describes the chemical substance called dopamine, the brain cells that produce dopamine, and the pathways in the brain along which dopamine travels.

"I began by asking myself some questions. Why are the elderly more susceptible to depression? It is not a complete explanation to say that old age is a season of losses and the period of general decline of health, because about 75 percent of older people manage these troubles without clinical symptoms of depressed mood, sadness, or reduced activity. So there must be another reason. We know now that the chemical cause of so many symptoms of aging is in the brain — that the neurotransmitters are less alert in carrying messages from neuron to neuron." Dopamine is one of those neurotransmitters and, according to Knoll, the degradation of dopamine is in all likelihood one of the culprits in age-related depression.

"I asked myself why there is an age-related decrease in sexual vigor. Sexual activity is known to be influenced by many factors, like good health, stable marriage, satisfactory sexual partner, adequate financial and social status, and the like. But even in the males who meet all the requirements for retention and maintenance of sexual functioning, there is an age-related decrease in sexual vigor. Why is that? Because we are getting old? Yes, that is the simple answer. But why is there such a variation in sexual activity among various age groups? We know that median coital activity is greatest in men between 30 and 34 and decreases progressively with increasing age. But why, even in the age group 65-69, are there men who have higher frequencies of sexual activity than men in the 30-34 age group? It is well-known from animal experiments that the dopaminergic system facilitates coital activity in males.

"And now we have learned over the past 25 years that a lack of dopamine is associated with the frequent appearance of Parkinson's disease in the latter stages of life. So the dopaminergic system has a role in three age-related phenomena: depression, declining sexual activity, and Parkinson's disease. That is why I call the dopaminergic system the engine of life."

Knoll lives at 4/B Jaszai Mari Terrace in an apartment building separated from the Danube by a leafy square. It is in a neighborhood that was the home of Budapest's intelligentsia before the war. His apartment is large by Budapest standards, about 130 square meters, and is tastefully decorated with contemporary Hungarian art. His first wife, a historian who wrote a book on Hungarian fascism, died many years ago. His present wife, Berta, is a warm, gentle woman who was once his student.

It is a far cry from the life he led in his childhood.

Knoll was born in Kispest, one of a number of surrounding towns that was absorbed into Budapest in 1948. On the outskirts of the city, near Ferihegy Airport, Kispest remains as an industrial suburb, its neighborhoods of small, modest homes interspersed with factories.

"My father was a hardworking man, very simple, not educated. He was a very, very religious orthodox

59

Jew who was educated in Hebrew, but his Hungarian was not so perfect and he collected money for a big firm that sold sugar, flour, and chocolate. He worked very hard. He was a very simple man, but very clever. And he had always the older Jewish habit that he only had a respect for knowing something — learning — like they learn the Talmud. He always told my brother and me that we had to learn and learn and learn. My mother was educated. She spoke German. I spoke German with my mother. I spoke Yiddish with my father. And I spoke Hungarian with my brother."

Somewhere in this childhood was the root of his ambition to be a doctor. Although he has never practiced medicine, he says, "I am a medical doctor. I'm a physician. I think as a physician and I worked as a physician. But I'm working in another place." That "other place" is the mind, or rather, the brain.

"Ever since I was a medical student I have had the idea that everything depends on the activation of the brain. So we have to study how the brain is getting active; what happens in the brain; what can be done to change what happens in the brain; and so on."

Knoll follows a strict routine. He arrives at his office at 8:30 a.m. and stays until 6:30 p.m. In the evenings he works at home, writing. Was it his work, the sheer volume of it, that caused his heart attack?

Knoll remembers the day. It happened on October 8, 1984, while he was driving to collect an honorary degree at Magdeburg University in Germany. Being a doctor, he knew what it was. Being human, he kept hoping it was just a severe attack of angina. He had bypass surgery almost two years later on July 10, 1986, at Harvard Medical School.

"No, it was not my work. I believe the cause was

when I was very young. I suffered very much in the war. I was transported to a Nazi concentration camp — you have heard the name Auschwitz. I was escorted to this concentration camp in June 1944 with my parents, who were killed there. And, after just a few weeks in there, I was mishandled by the SS, who usually killed most of the people they could. But I survived."

There were more than one million Jews in Hungary before the Second World War. There are now said to be somewhere between 50,000 and 80,000, although that estimate falls far short of the true number. Even today, in Hungary, Jews do not wear their religion on their sleeves. Budapest, shortly after the turn of the century, was sometimes referred to by Hungarian nationalists as "Judapest" because of the accomplishments of Jewish Hungarians in the arts and professions. In 1910, although Jews constituted less than five percent of Hungary's population, nearly half of the country's doctors, lawyers, and journalists were Jewish. They dominated the culture in Hungary so much so that, with the rise of a new kind of nationalism that found its ultimate personification in Hitler, they were all the more the victims of anti-Semitism.

Knoll was herded into the first of five concentration camps at the age of 14. His most vivid memories begin with his arrival at Auschwitz in the spring of 1944. His parents and older brother embarked from one side of a railroad cattle car, he from the other. Knoll never saw them again.

"After four months in Auschwitz, in September 1944, I was removed to another concentration camp near Berlin. It was a very cold winter. It was a very terrible place, and for two days and nights I was tied to a post. Then I went to Buchenwald, which is a very,

61

very famous place. There I spent only one day.

"That was the last period of the war. From Buchenwald they sent us by train through Czechoslovakia for 21 days, just to avoid the liberating troops. That was the most important thing for them — to somehow keep the concentration camp people. Crazy. We were 21 days without food. There were 65 of us in one train wagon. Two survived.

"I arrived at Dachau and my mind was completely clear. One suffers only four days: I suffered only four days from hunger. After that I survived. I was 37 kilograms. And that was, I believe, on April 27, 1945. I never talk about that because I think it's very personal.

"On the day the American troops liberated Dachau, I remember I lay on that wooden bed. I couldn't, of course, move or talk, because I was like a skeleton. But my mind was completely clear, which I still don't understand. And then the first troops, mostly black people, came. They were very kind to all of us. They immediately gave us loaves of bread and pieces of meat and so on. Weeks and weeks went by, and regular troops came. I remember the captain, and even his name. And so they gave us anything you can imagine. At midnight, even, we could eat.

"So, slowly I recovered, and later I got an edema (a buildup of water in the body's tissues). What was very odd was that it was in the gut, in the cavity just above the diaphragm. So they had to remove the water weekly, and I had the edema for two and a half years. And . . . so I think that was what caused the blocks in the heart, because I had that plaque. I think the plaque that caused the heart attack developed in that period.

"I will tell you just one short story about the tension. It happened the one day I was in Buchenwald. An acid smell was behind. There were four of us. And the man behind, the Nazi, just for fun, shot one of us. And then he shot the second man, and the third. But I managed to survive. I believe it was because I didn't turn around. I didn't look behind. I'm sure of that, because I have no other explanation. When I heard the first shot, I didn't care. Probably I survived for that reason, because I didn't care — I didn't look behind. A man's life had a lower value than a piece of furniture. And, believe me, when millions die and there is no more life, man is without value in nature."

Knoll pauses for a moment to contemplate the phenomenon of Hitler. "After thousands and thousands of years of the development of human society, Hitler still subscribed to the most cruel laws of nature. He thought that only the strong should survive, and that to win the battle we have to kill those who are of no value. Darwin understood the laws of nature, but he also knew they could not be used against human society.

"The law of nature is simple. There is a built-in mechanism. We don't know the reason. We don't know how it works. Medieval man called it the power of life. If we can change that mechanism, that system, we can protect ourselves from avoidable age-related decline."

One of the first discoveries of psychopharmacology was that there was a connection between age-related depression and the wearing out of the brain's communications system. The chemical substances that carry messages among the neurons of the brain are either diminished, or else they cease to function efficiently.

We have also learned in the past 25 years that a deficiency in one of the brain's message-carrying chemicals — dopamine — is associated with the frequent appearance of parkinsonism in the latter stages of life. Dopamine plays an important role in those parts of the brain that are known to control motor function. But it also travels to other parts of the brain — to the limbic system, which affects emotions, and to the cortex, where it may affect memory, intellect, and personality.

Knoll believes this highly branched dopaminergic system may be the source of our active reflexes, our inner drives. He believes that deprenyl, because it protects the section of the brain that produces dopamine, may have a protective effect on the decay of the brain. If that is so further investigations into the nature of Parkinson's disease should prove enlightening. After all, Parkinson's is the neurodegenerative disease we know most about.

4

THE WORLD OF
PARKINSON'S DISEASE

THREE HUNDRED EXPECTANT PEOPLE came to the meeting in Toronto. Long before 7:30 p.m. they began to file into the main-floor auditorium of a downtown building, acknowledging those they knew and sometimes saying hello to strangers. Acquaintances or not, there was an air of camraderie. A woman, one of the volunteers, opened the proceedings. "We're just delighted that you're here," she said. "I've had the pleasure of meeting a number of you and I hope to meet more of you." The woman spoke not in patronizing terms, as if to a group of young children, but in simple, caring language. She talked about an upcoming party — "we look forward to a fun evening" — a daytime excursion, and other scheduled events. The audience was mature: that is to say, except for a scattering of young people, who appeared to be relatives, they were middle-aged or older. Many seemed normal. Others moved with a forward tilt, taking short, shuffling steps. Some were tremulous or had difficulty holding their heads steady. A few sat as if immobilized, shoulders bent grotesquely forward, mouths gaping.

There was a warm-up act. The man who came out of the audience was funny, with disheveled hair made all the more unruly because his head bobbed and weaved. "You'll have to excuse me," he said in a stage whisper, "but I've got Parkinson's." And everybody laughed.

This was a meeting of the Parkinson Foundation of Canada, a volunteer organization devoted to the support of research into the cause and cure of Parkinson's disease. The Canadian foundation, like its counterpart in the United States, the American Parkinson Disease Association, performs other very important functions: it encourages the formation of local support groups throughout the country and promotes exercise, counseling, and therapy sessions, as well as social get-togethers. In the past 25 years the encouragement and understanding of people with Parkinson's has grown into a huge nonprofit industry. Among its most valued services is providing information about new developments in the treatment of the disease because, when people with Parkinson's get together, the question they most often ask one another is: "What's the latest?"

Almost everyone knows someone who either has Parkinson's disease or is related to someone who has Parkinson's. The disease rarely surfaces before age 40. At age 50 the chances of becoming parkinsonian are one in a hundred, and at age 60 one in 50. There are believed to be almost one million sufferers in North America, perhaps 100,000 of them in Canada. In the United Kingdom it is variously said there are between 60,000 and 100,000 victims of Parkinson's disease.

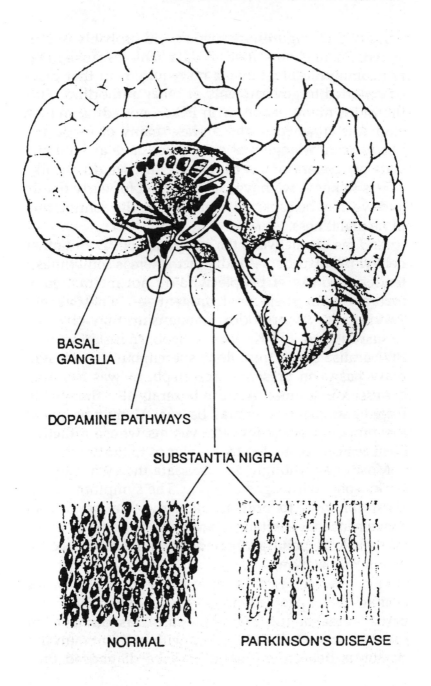

BASAL
GANGLIA

DOPAMINE PATHWAYS

SUBSTANTIA NIGRA

NORMAL   PARKINSON'S DISEASE

All of these figures are suspect and probably understated. There is no statistical data bank: because PD is not communicable, there is no requirement that cases be reported to governments or other authorities. Furthermore, many people with PD do not admit to it. A stigma is attached to the disease: many of us do not like to acknowledge that our bodies have arrived at a state of accelerated functional decline; we do not like others to know we have been marked for early death; and we may be especially sensitive to the connotation of mental illness.

And the line between the symptoms of PD and other behavioral disorders is indistinct. There is sometimes a tendency to say of people who do not interact comfortably with their environment — "They've got Parkinson's." Unorthodox mannerisims may give rise to suspicions of PD. Katherine Hepburn is said to have PD because of her tremulous speech, but that idosyncrasy has been present since Hepburn was a young actress. Muhammad Ali, the boxer, is also thought to have Parkinson's. That may be true: Ali may be one of the proportionately few PD victims whose affliction has been caused by too many bumps to the head.

Most of all, though, we associate the symptoms of Parkinson's with signs of aging. The symptom that is most common to both is akinesia — a paucity of movement that is often reflected in a slowing of activities such as getting dressed, getting out of bed or chairs, and walking.

Parkinsonism is the name given to a syndrome manifested by people who have sustained damage in a certain area of the brain. Because this damage, or "lesion," cannot be identified with certainty until a person is dead, the disease may be diagnosed only through the presence of characteristic symptoms, and even then only by a physician experienced in observing or treating PD.

Sometimes there is an identifiable reason that a person becomes parkinsonian. The condition may be caused, at any age, by a stroke, repeated blows to the head, metal poisoning, or drug overdose. Or a person may become parkinsonian for no apparent reason.

It is convenient to divide parkinsonism into four categories. One is miscellaneous: the syndrome may result, as in the case of Muhammad Ali, from a blow or repeated blows to the head, or from cerebral arteriosclerosis, or from the ingestion of poisons such as carbon monoxide. A second category is postencephalitic. In this category, now almost extinct, the syndrome followed in the wake of an epidemic of encephalitis in the 1920s. A third category, detected only during the past three decades, is the parkinsonism that is induced by drugs. These types of parkinsonism represent by far the minority of cases.

The fourth category of Parkinson's disease is by far the most common. It is called *idiopathic* PD — it just happens. The cause of the degeneration of brain cells, which occurs at a faster rate than in normal humans, is unknown. Idiopathic PD may occur in adults of any age, but it is unusual before age 40, and it happens increasingly with advancing years.

The symptoms common to all forms of the disease are tremor, which usually occurs when a person is at rest; rigidity, or stiffness of the skeletal muscles; akinesia, difficulty in initiating or modifying movement; and problems in maintaining or adjusting posture. Often there is a short, unsteady gait, mask-like facial expression, or distortion or faintness in speech. Less obvious symptoms are excessive perspiration, increased salivation leading to drooling, and intolerance to heat. The muscles are not numb or paralyzed; they just lack direction from the brain.

Tremor is the most obvious symptom, and is often the first to be detected. More disabling, and sometimes even more embarrassing, is the impairment of voluntary movement. The chronicles of Parkinson's disease cannot begin to include all the stories of people afraid to leave their homes for fear of being seized by an unchecked dance of movement or, just as embarrassing, by a catatonic or frozen state.

Because of the array of symptoms, only one or two of which may be present in the early stages, Parkinson's is not easy to diagnose. There are other, similar, neurologic disturbances that affect motor function. And then there are injuries to parts of the brain not primarily concerned with motor function that may nonetheless affect efficiency of movement.

One of the most confusing things about Parkinson's is that it is one of the very few progressive diseases that is often preceded by persistent good health.

Roger Caron is a case in point. "I've always been so incredibly healthy," he says with emphasis.

Caron spends as much time as he can working out in the gymnasium. He has been lifting weights for 35 years and says proudly, "I don't look nearly as old as 52."

One day in 1983 he noticed that his gym bag, which he always carried in his left hand, was banging against his thigh. It was the strangest thing. As time went on, he noticed another phenomenon: his left hand kept reaching into his trouser pocket. "It was like there was a magnet in there," he says.

Caron, who lives in Ottawa, visited his local doctor. "You've had some kind of a stroke," he was told. "You'd better see a neurologist."

Ottawa is separated by the Ottawa River from the city of Hull in the neighboring province of Quebec. The neurologist whom Caron visited had her office in Hull. "It was a dingy, dreary place," he remembers, and the neurologist "reminded me of those Hildas you read about who worked in concentration camps."

"Hilda," or whatever her name was, "noticed that my feet were tapping on the floor and that I never blinked my eyes. She looked me straight in the face and said, 'You've got Parkinson's disease.' My reaction? I was real sad."

Caron knows how to tell a story. In fact, he has told stories in four books, the first of which — *Go-Boy!* — has sold more than 700,000 copies. *Go-Boy!* is a true account of Caron's time in jail, where he has spent a total of 24 years for bank robberies. Before he became so widely known as an author, he was infamous for having escaped from jail 13 times, a record in Canada.

He has been on the outside for quite a few years now, still working out daily at the gym, and still writing. He remembers vividly the weeks following his diagnosis of Parkinson's disease. "I'd always been in such good shape. I was like a superman. But when I'd be talking to someone and I had to concentrate, I just felt like screaming. I just couldn't believe I had Parkinson's."

It is probable that Caron got Parkinson's about 10 years before he was diagnosed, following a knife fight with a prisoner in Kingston Penitentiary, one of Canada's maximum-security prisons. He refused to snitch on his fellow inmate and, as punishment, was sent to a hospital for the mentally insane. There he was given a sedative drug that, he learned later, is capable of inducing Parkinson's disease. "I don't know what the drug was — I was just a kid then — but every time they gave it to me I got muscle spasms and shook all over."

It reminded him of the film *One flew over the Cuckoo's Nest* in which so many of the asylum inmates exhibit parkinsonian symptoms after being fed a diet of sedative pills by the nurse in the film.[1]

If there was such a thing as parkinsonism before the disease was first clinically identified in the nineteenth century, then the symptoms were ascribed to rheumatism or some other affliction — or even to insanity. Then, in 1817, the first clinical description of the disease was given by Dr. James Parkinson.

Little is known about Parkinson. The son of a surgeon, he was born in 1755 and practiced medicine in Shoreditch, then a pastoral English village and now part of the sprawling metropolitan area of Greater London. The precious few reminiscences of the village doctor describe him as "rather below middle stature with an energetic, intelligent, and pleasant countenance and of mild and courteous manner." He was interested in chemistry, geology, and paleontology, and he wrote many articles on medical matters.

One of those articles was called "An Essay on the Shaking Palsy":

> The disease, respecting which the present inquiry is made, is of a nature highly afflictive.

---

[1]Caron's symptoms of Parkinson's disease have not put a stop to his daily weight-lifting. He has slurred speech, and the other symptoms mainly affect the left side of his body. The more disabling effects were neurotic: for a while recurrent anxiety attacks threatened to put an end to his writing career.

Notwithstanding which, it has not yet obtained a place in the classification of nosologists; some have regarded its characteristic symptoms as distinct and different diseases, and others have given its name to diseases differing essentially from it; while the unhappy sufferer has considered it as an evil, from the domination of which he has no prospect of escape.

Parkinson described the symptoms of the disease that was to bear his name as "involuntary tremulous motion, with lessened muscular power, in parts not in action and even when supported; with a propensity to bend the trunk forward, and to pass from a walking to a running pace; the sense and intellects being uninjured."

His description was uncannily accurate, except — and just perhaps — for his assertion that "the sense and the intellects (are) uninjured." In this regard he may have been mistaken: it is now estimated that about 25 percent of PD victims suffer from at least some impairment in memory and cognition. Whether these dementias are a symptom of Parkinson's, or are caused by depression or anxiety, or are simply outriders of the aging process, is not known.

During James Parkinson's time there was little search for relief from the disease for the simple reason that it most often afflicted older people. As Parkinson said, "Seldom occurring before the age of 50, and frequently yielding but little inconvenience for several months, it is generally considered as the irremediable diminution of the nervous influence, naturally resulting from declining life; and remedies therefore are seldom sought for."

For almost 100 years after Parkinson wrote "An Essay on the Shaking Palsy," there were no worthwhile treatments for the disease. The despair was voiced by Alfred Tennyson, who asked in his poem "The Two Voices," "What drug can make a withered palsy cease to shake?"

Parkinson had speculated that the disease involved some disturbance in the brain stem. He was correct. When a young doctor named Tretiakoff opened the brains of nine PD victims in 1919, he found that all nine suffered damage to an area called the substantia nigra.

Decay of the cells in the substantia nigra is now recognized as the condition of the body that results in Parkinson's disease. That, however, is only one of the clues to the cause of the disease — its *aetiology*. What has so far escaped detection is the reason the lesion occurs in the brain's substantia nigra.

The prevalence of the disease, among a people or in a community at some special time, has opened up some interesting avenues of research, which so far have led to dead ends. Parkinson's disease may be found anywhere in the world. It does not favor either sex, and studies with twins suggest it is almost certainly not hereditary. There is no conclusive evidence that the incidence of the disease varies according to race or skin color.

Diet has been examined as a possible factor in PD, as has the environment. The most widely publicized study of the possible influence of environmental factors was conducted by neurologist Andre Barbeau, the founder of the Clinical Research Institute in Montreal, Canada. In 1985 Barbeau announced that the highest concentration of people in the Province of Quebec suffering from Parkinson's disease lived either in the vicinity of pulp and paper mills or close to garden farming areas. From this, Barbeau deduced that pollutants — fungicides in pulp and paper mills, pesticides in gardening areas — might be the trigger for PD. His case has never been proven, yet the suspicions raised by his study reinforce the theory that the disease is caused by an external poison that finds its way to the substantia nigra.

All of the parkinsonian symptoms, or at least all of those that can be detected by simple observation, were evident at the Parkinson Foundation of Canada meeting in Toronto. There are six stages of Parkinson's disease, and there were people there representing all but one — or maybe two. There were people in Stage 1, in which the disease affects only one side of the body. There were people in Stage 2, in which the disease affects both sides of the body. There were people in Stage 3, where the disease impairs balance or walking. There were people in Stage 4, where maintaining balance and walking are so difficult that a wheelchair is required. And there were probably people in Stage 0, but they could not be identified because in Stage 0 there are no visible symptoms of the disease. The one category that was definitely not represented was Stage 5. In Stage 5, the most serious stage, the patient is completely immobile and almost certainly bedridden.

This was a very special meeting. It was, first of all, the beginning of the annual Parkinson Awareness Week, and the event had been advertised in Toronto's newspapers. The air of expectation was heightened by the imminent arrival of a very special guest — Dr. Anthony Lang, head of the department of neurology at Toronto Western Hospital. Every seat was filled, and extra chairs had to be provided.

Tony Lang is about 40 years old, moderately shorter than average, with a neat mustache. Lang has his own neurology practice, is the head of the movement disorders clinic at his hospital, and frequently lectures to students and staff at medical schools. He has published 50 papers, most of them dealing with Parkinson's disease, and has won many awards. To the people in the audience, Lang was a person whose raiment was to be touched at the hem.

Almost everyone there had at least a rudimentary understanding that the symptoms of PD were a response to a lack of dopamine in the brain. Lang knew that his listeners were familiar with the dopamine deficit, but he also knew they never tired of having it explained to them.

It so happens that, of all the cells in the body, those that produce dopamine — the dopaminergic — age faster than any others. The average person starts to lose dopamine at about age 45, and thereafter the normal supply of this chemical transmitter diminishes by about 13 percent each decade. If there were such a thing as a dopamine fuel gauge, we would find that our reservoir of dopamine was only 87 percent full by age 55, 74 percent full by age 65, and so on until it was only 22 percent full by age 105. Once our dopamine resources reach the level of about 20 percent, we start to exhibit the symptoms of Parkinson's disease. Most of us do not reach age 105, so most of us do not get Parkinson's disease. The people who are afflicted by PD are the ones who have an accelerated loss of dopaminergic cells. Their dopamine resources fall to the critical twenty percent level at a much earlier age.

"We can think," Lang said at the meeting, "of the loss of cells in that very critical area of the brain that

I'm sure most of you know about, the substantia nigra, that little black area in what's called the midbrain. It is normal for cells to die with age. So, as we all grow older, we lose cells, particularly in that area but also in many other areas of the nervous system, as well.

"We know you can get along with about 80 percent loss of those cells in the substantia nigra before you begin to show the signs of the disease. So it's thought that the disease has been present probably for many years before any of you ever arrived at your doctor's office with the shaking or the slowness or whatever you were complaining about at the time.

"Now if we're going to do anything about developing preventative therapies, ideally one would want to know who's going to develop Parkinson's disease before they ever show the symptoms. But, unfortunately, we don't have a test yet. We don't know the cause. We don't have any clue whether myself or anyone else who doesn't demonstrate the disease may develop it in the future. I may have been exposed to the cause. It may have been a toxin, or it may have been something I ate or something I was exposed to. I may develop the disease in another ten years. If I could determine that — if I could determine I was at risk — I could take a medication that might prevent me from reaching that critical level where I've lost 80 percent of my dopaminergic cells."

When Lang finished speaking, the first question they asked him was: "What about deprenyl?" The answer was that deprenyl was a name for a drug not yet available in Canada. It was sold in different countries under various names — in Hungary it was Jumex; in Great Britain it was Eldepryl.

Lang is a cautious man, always careful not to raise

expectations. Therefore he said ". . . deprenyl is a unique drug. It may slow down the death of the cells that produce dopamine. The critical question is whether deprenyl will slow down the progression of the disease."[2]

---

[2]Five years later, the results of the DATATOP study proved deprenyl does slow the progression of Parkinson's disease and, in addition, it protects the brain's dopaminergic system.

5

THE PROMISE OF LEVODOPA

ANY ONE OF A NUMBER OF SCIENTISTS might have won the Nobel prize in medicine or physiology for developing the use of the wonder drug levodopa in the treatment of Parkinson's disease. None did, perhaps because there were so many people involved in the process. Or maybe it was because, in retrospect, the achievement seemed to flow so logically from a mounting number of intriguing clues.

The first clue, which meant nothing by itself, turned up in 1955 when it was accidentally discovered that an ancient Indian remedy called reserpine could induce parkinsonian symptoms. The other clues arose from the discovery that a substance called dopamine was one of the brain's important chemical neurotransmitters. Dopamine previously had attracted little attention from biologists. It was known to occur in several of the body's organs, but it was not detected in the brain until 1957. When its primary location in the brain was traced to the basal ganglia — masses of gray matter responsible for the programming of normal movement — then it seemed that dopamine, or maybe the lack of it, might have something to do with Parkinson's disease.

During the late 1950s, a number of scientists in the United States, Austria, Sweden, England, and Canada were on the trail of dopamine. The fact that they were all pursuing the same avenues of investigation had a lot to do with the recent development of powerful new instruments such as the spectrophotofluorimeter, which allowed them to observe the movements of tiny molecules within the body.

These scientists either knew one another — or they were aware of one another's work through the medium of scientific journals. In this loose brotherhood, the closer they came to finding the pathological cause of dopamine, the more they competed for recognition.

In 1959 Oleh Hornykiewicz knew as much as anyone about dopamine. Its existence had been recognized since early in the century, but there was much debate about whether it was really important. Scientists were unwilling to assign any particular role to dopamine, even though it showed up in the heart, lungs, kidneys, liver, stomach, intestines, and elsewhere in the body. Dopamine was an amine, a derivative of one of the amino acids that are sometimes called the building blocks of proteins. After years of argument, some people had started to admit that maybe dopamine acted as a go-between in the body's chemical synthesis of other amines, such as adrenaline and noradrenaline. Adrenaline had long been known for its importance as an "activator" to prepare the body for fight or flight; noradrenaline, among other things, helped to regulate circulation. But hardly anyone believed that dopamine, by itself, was really very important. Oleh Hornykiewicz believed otherwise.

In 1959 Hornykiewicz was a young pharmacology professor at the University of Vienna. He had just returned from Oxford, where he had been a scholarship student under the supervision of Dr. Herman Blaschko. For many years Blaschko had been alone in arguing that dopamine had its own purpose — its own physiological role in the body. Blaschko, many years before, had been the first to postulate that dopamine was involved in the synthesis of adrenaline and noradrenaline. It took a long time for his colleagues to accept his theory, and now that it was proven correct, Blaschko's fellow scientists were every bit as reluctant to embrace his argument that dopamine might have some further significance in the body.

At Oxford Hornykiewicz had been turned loose on dopamine by his mentor, Blaschko. Studying the effects of dopamine on the blood pressure of guinea pigs, he concluded that, whereas noradrenaline increased blood pressure, dopamine *reduced* it, thus proving that dopamine was not simply a chemical intermediary in the formation of noradrenaline but that it had its own independent physiological function. Hornykiewicz's conclusions formed the basis for his first important scientific paper, which was published in the *British Journal of Pharmacology*. It was the first published article to demonstrate that dopamine was important in its own right. His scholarship over, Hornykiewicz returned to Vienna.

Reserpine, the Indian herbal remedy, is one of the more famous substances in drug folklore. It had been used for hundreds of years in southern Asia to treat a wide variety of disorders, including snakebite and mental disease. When reserpine was finally introduced into Western medicine in the early 1950s, it was because of the drug's antihypertensive properties. All other drugs that had previously been used to treat high blood pressure acted by dilating the blood vessels; reserpine was the first to exert its antihypertensive influence by its effect on the brain. Soon, however, reserpine became more widely used as a sedative, becoming the model for the new word *tranquilizer.*

Reserpine was very popular, not only with patients who benefited from its soothing qualities, but also with scientists who became fascinated with some of its peculiar influences on brain function. Its side effects, and the development of superior antipsychotic drugs, spelled its demise. Reserpine's greatest danger was that it sometimes precipitated depression severe enough to lead to suicide. A less unpleasant side effect was that it could provoke involuntary and abnormal movements, which are described as extrapyramidal, one of the hallmarks of Parkinson's disease They are so described because they are *not* under the control of the brain's pyramidal system.

The pyramidal system is related to voluntary movement — it obeys a person's will. The term derives its name from the large, pyramid-shaped cells in the cortex of the brain which, when excited, send motor impulses to the spinal cord, from whence the signals are transmitted to various parts of the body to contract the appropriate muscles.

For example, we perform a pyramidal function when we innervate the muscles of the larynx in order to speak. But if we concomitantly move our hands, for emphasis or to make ourselves understood more clearly, such movements are subconscious and are called "associated" or "extrapyramidal" movements.

It is within the extrapyramidal system of the brain that the basal ganglia resides, and within the basal ganglia the substantia nigra, whose decay is the pathological sign of Parkinson's disease. When the cells of the substantia nigra fail to produce sufficient dopamine, the body becomes parkinsonian.

In the mid-1950s scientists knew that reserpine induced extrapyramidal symptoms, and they also knew that extrapyramidal functions were within the control and regulation of the basal ganglia. One might have deduced, therefore, that reserpine somehow caused an interference in the basal ganglia, but at the time there was no connecting link. It was known that the reason reserpine was useful in psychiatry, as a sedative or tranquilizer, was because it depleted certain substances in the brain. But it was not known that it depleted dopamine, because at the time no on knew that dopamine existed in the brain. Nor did anyone know that dopamine was produced by the cells of the substantia nigra and that it was the essential means of communication orchestrated by the basal ganglia.

Quite apart from the reserpine phenomenon, an Englishwoman named Kathleen Miontagu made the discovery in 1957 that dopamine was present in the brain. A short time later Swedish scientists led by Arvid Carlsson demonstrated that reserpine could deplete dopamine in the brain. Still later, in 1959, two scientists from Carlsson's laboratory at the University of Göteborg determined that the richest concentration of dopamine in the brains of dogs was in the basal ganglia and that dopamine was "thus concerned with central motor function."

Those were the pieces of information from which Oleh Hornykiewicz deduced that people suffering from Parkinson's disease might have a shortage of dopamine in the region of the brain's basal ganglia. In the summer of 1989 at the Institute for Biological Pharmacology in the hospital district of Vienna, Hornykiewicz recalled the events that followed.

"When I read that report — which showed that in the dog brain dopamine was concentrated in the basal ganglia, I immediately realized there was something very interesting. Because I knew what dopamine was, I felt it had its own function in the body because of the experiments Blaschko had made me do, and I was very much aware that reserpine produced symptoms that were very similar to what one sees in Parkinson's patients. And that is where my work began in Parkinson's disease."

Hornykiewicz is shorter than average, amiable, and very precise. In his office he wore a tweed jacket over a professorial gray cardigan. But he no longer teaches. He and his family spent ten years in Canada, beginning in 1967, and although he now makes his home in Vienna, he remains a visiting professor at the departments of pharmacology and psychiatry at the University of Toronto as well as head of the human brain laboratory at Toronto's Clarke Institute of Psychiatry.

In 1959 Hornykiewicz, then 32, set out to prove his theory that people with Parkinson's disease had a shortage of dopamine in the basal ganglia. The only way to prove that theory was to examine the brains of deceased patients.

Hornykiewicz needed two kinds of brains. First, he would have to acquire normal ones, which would serve as "controls," to see whether the distribution of dopamine was similar in humans to that in dogs and other animals. Control brains are not difficult to come by, and Hornykiewicz ascertained that the dopamine in human brains was highly concentrated in the basal ganglia. But the pharmacologist also needed parkinsonian brains to see whether dopamine was missing from the basal ganglia. He found the second type of brain at a large senior citizens' home in Lainz, near Vienna, where the head of the neurological ward was Dr. Walter Birkmayer, who would be his colleague in the development of levodopa and who would, many years later, be the first person to use deprenyl in the treatment of Parkinson's disease.

Conducting human brain autopsies was a novel pursuit in 1959. The whole study of the physiology of the brain was in its infancy. Also, it was not known whether unstable chemicals, such as dopamine, could survive the postmortem waiting period stipulated by law before a body's organs may be removed.

Hornykiewicz obtained his first Parkinson's brain from Lainz, courtesy of Dr. Birkmayer, in April 1959. As he suspected, the brain was almost bereft of dopamine. After examining five more brains in the succeeding 14 months, he was ready to publish. His historical paper, showing that dopamine was absent from the brains of people with Parkinson's disease, appeared in German in the December 1960 issue of *Wiener Klinische Wochenschrift*.

The discovery of dopamine deficiency in the brains of patients with Parkinson's disease was of crucial importance because (a) it demonstrated that genuine Parkinson's disease had basically the same neurochemical disorder as the parkinsonlike condition induced by the drug reserpine, (b) it provided support for the notion that dopamine played a physiological role in the control of extrapyramidal motor function, and (c) it suggested, for the first time, the possibility that the lack of a simple chemical in a well-defined brain center may be responsible for the clinical manifestations in a chronic, degenerative brain disease.

Even before his article appeared in *Klinische Wochenschrift*, it occurred to Hornykiewicz that if a lack of dopamine were the cause of Parkinson's disease, then replacement of the dopamine might possibly remove or relieve the symptoms of the disease.

Dopamine can be synthesized in the laboratory, but it is not capable of crossing the blood-brain barrier, the name for the system of structures and cells that selectively prevents certain substances from entering the brain. Hornykiewicz decided that a way around this problem might be to introduce levodopa into the body. Levodopa, which was dopamine's immediate chemical precursor, *was* capable of crossing the blood-brain barrier. Once in the brain, levodopa would be metabolized to dopamine.

To test his theory, Hornykiewicz needed to try out levodopa on Parkinson's patients. Once again he visited Dr. Birkmayer, who had several PD patients under his care.

But first of all there was the problem of an inadequate supply of levodopa. The chemical was expensive to produce, and was only available in very small quantities, certainly not sufficient for oral doses. With the tiny amount of levodopa at his disposal, Hornykiewicz decided to take the intravenous route. Birkmayer, who was experienced in observing the effects of drugs, was the man to conduct the trials, and he injected 20 Parkinson's patients with the intravenous levodopa solution.

In June 1961 there was an excited telephone call from Birkmayer. "This is a wonder drug!" he exclaimed to Hornykiewicz. "I injected it and the patients who couldn't get up from a sitting position can now walk and jump and . . ."

The first published report that levodopa was highly efficacious in the treatment of Parkinson's disease appeared in November 1961. The co-authors were Hornykiewicz and Birkmayer:

> The effect of a single intravenous administration of levodopa was, in summary, a complete abolition or substantial relief of akiensia. Bedridden patients who were unable to sit up, patients who could not stand up from a sitting position, and patients who, when standing, could not start walking, performed all these activities after levodopa with ease. They walked around with normal associated movements and they could even run and jump. The voiceless, aphonic speech, blurred by palilalia and unclear articulation, became forceful and clear again as in a normal person. For short periods of time the patients were able to perform motor activities that could not be prompted by any comparable degree by any other known drug. This "dopa" effect reached its peak within two to three hours and lasted, in diminishing intensity, for 24 hours. In some patients, especially in milder cases, the motor activation persisted for even longer periods of time. So far we

observed this effect in all examined patients
with parkinsonism (20 cases), although to a
different degree . . .

Those startling conclusions appeared in German in a
local Viennese medical journal.[1] For all that it mattered
to the hundreds of thousands of people suffering from
Parkinson's disease, the article might never have
appeared at all. It was to be several years before
levodopa became known to the world as a miracle
treatment.

Months before that first article on the use of
levodopa in the treatment of Parkinson's disease, a
group of scientists three thousand miles away were
arriving at the same conclusions. Theodore Sourkes at
the University of Montreal and his colleague Andre
Barbeau at Montreal's Clinical Research Institute had
shown that levels of dopamine were significantly lower than normal in humans with Parkinson's disease.
They were about to embark on the next stage of their
investigation — an analysis of postmortem brains —
when they found out this work had already been
carried out in Vienna.

Barbeau, a 29-year-old neurologist, had made the
same deductions as Hornykiewicz. If a lack of dopamine caused the symptoms of Parkinson's disease,
then replacement of the missing dopamine might relieve symptoms of the disease. He proceeded to try
levodopa on six of his patients. The results, as he was
later to discover, were similar to those in the clinical

---

[1]"The Effect of L-3, 4-Dihydroxyphenylalanine (=Dopa) on Akinesia in Parkinsonism," Birkmayer, W. and Hornykiewicz, O., *Wiener Klinische Wochenschrift*, Vol.
73, 787-88 (Vienna: Springer-Verlag, 1961).

trials conducted by Hornykiewicz and Birkmayer. But there had been one significant procedural difference. Barbeau was able to obtain sufficient levodopa so he could administer oral dosages.

Barbeau decided he would announce his findings at the World Neurology congress in Rome in September 1961. On his way home he planned to stop over in Vienna to introduce himself to Oleh Hornykiewicz, the man he knew had conducted the postmortem brain examinations.

Hornykiewicz remembered that summer: "Andre wrote me a letter that he would be in Rome and that he would like to come and meet me. In Vienna he showed me an abstract of what he had presented to the congress — showing the effect of levodopa in Parkinson's patients. I learned that he had done the same work in Montreal, completely independently. We didn't know of each other. I didn't know that he was doing it, and he could not possibly have known that we were doing it here in Vienna."

Relations between Hornykiewicz and Barbeau were cordial and without jealousy, both at that first meeting in Vienna and afterward.

"We had lunch at an outdoor café, a very pleasant lunch," Hornykiewicz recalled. "And Dr. Birkmayer came along. It was a very nice day, and I had the impression that Andre was a very lively person with lots of ideas. I can still see him sitting opposite me — he was very stout. Andre was a very active person who liked to talk about science. He gave me the impression that he was really an excellent clinician — an excellent observer."

The two men sitting in the sunshine in Vienna, Hornykiewicz and Barbeau, knew they had made an important discovery. They had shown the importance of dopamine in the function of the basal ganglia and, most importantly, they had found a drug that would prove to be of invaluable benefit to patients suffering from the disabling disease of Parkinson's. But they never got the credit that was their due.

Both Hornykiewicz and Barbeau made before-and-after films of their patients that showed the reviving effects of levodopa. Between 1961 and 1965 both men published a number of articles describing the way levodopa reawakened the muscles of inert Parkinson's patients. They had established the scientific fact that a lack of dopamine in the basal ganglia was the culprit in Parkinson's disease, and they had demonstrated that levodopa, by substituting for the depleted stores of dopamine, could restore the motor functions of people with PD. Hornykiewicz tried to persuade others to use levodopa, and so did Barbeau.

Pharmaceutical companies were interested, but not so much that any of them prepared supplies of the drug in commercial quantities. For years doctors failed to see the benefits of levodopa treatment. If they were able to detect any improvement in their patients after administering levodopa, they regarded it as transient. Some small clinical studies returned positive findings; the results of others were negative.

As extraordinary as this seems, it illustrates the capricious nature of the symptoms of PD as well as, among other things, the inexperience of doctors and others in the early 1960s in detecting and classifying changes in the condition of people with Parkinson's disease. It also illustrates the importance of administering the right dosages of a drug.

Hornykiewicz and Barbeau had not given nearly high enough dosages.

Several years after that lunch in Vienna, on May 8, 1967, an article deep in the back pages of the *New York Times* carried the following headline: PARKINSON'S VICTIMS REPORTED RELIEVED BY DRUG IN TESTS. A Dr. George Cotzias had reported to the Association of American Physicians that 26 Parkinson's patients had shown varying degrees of improvement after treatment with dopa. (Dopa is the racemic or unrefined form of levodopa.) Cotzias, who worked at the Brookhaven National Laboratory, part of the Atomic Energy Commission, had prepared a film that showed patients who had become self-sufficient and ambulatory when previously they could neither walk nor feed themselves.

Within a year the results of Cotzias's clinical trials were reported in the *Journal of the American Medical Association*. Cotzias was besieged by Parkinson's patients who wanted to take part in his ongoing trials, and a black market began to develop for levodopa. In 1970 the drug Sinemet, a levodopa preparation, was approved by the U.S. Food and Drug Administration within 30 days of application. Cotzias was acclaimed as the savior of Parkinson's patients everywhere.

George Cotzias was a very tall man with broad shoulders, a raconteur, a bon vivant who, after he became famed as the discoverer of levodopa therapy, occupied the best tables in the best restaurants, drank the choicest wines, and received the idolatrous attention of waiters.

Cotzias and his family had been refugees from Greece during World War II. His father had been mayor of Athens, his mother a famous hostess at literary

91

gatherings. As Cotzias later told the story, he was rejected by one American medical school after another because he could not speak English. According to his version, the Harvard Medical School allowed him to learn English and medicine at the same time. He graduated cum laude.

With levodopa Cotzias demonstrated that the secret of effective treatment was dosage. Too little, and the effects on patients were imperceptible to all but trained clinicians. Instead of milligrams Cotzias gave his patients grams — sometimes several times a day.

Cotzias arrived at his levodopa discovery from a different direction than that of Hornykiewicz and Barbeau. He had been convinced there was a connection between Parkinson's disease and the formation of skin pigmentation. When that theory proved to have no foundation, he decided to investigate the therapeutic potential of dopa. His intention, as he wrote at the time, was "to saturate (and keep saturating)" his patients with dopa. The technique of giving the dopa in gradually increasing doses up to quite large daily amounts proved to be successful and became the favored method of dosage.

Cotzias basked in his recognition as the discoverer of levodopa therapy. His failure to acknowledge the earlier achievements in Vienna and Montreal caused an estrangement with Hornykiewicz. Barbeau, himself not shy of publicity, was especially upset.

The names of nominees for the Nobel prize are never revealed, but it was known in the scientific community that the Nobel committee felt some recognition should be given for the development of levodopa therapy. Cotzias made no secret of the fact that he wanted the prize, and he had support from eminent neurologists in the United States. But what of Arvid Carlsson, the Swedish scientist whose laboratory had discovered the distribution of dopamine in the brain? And Hornykiewicz? Birkmayer? Barbeau?

In 1969, when the Lasker award, the highest American prize for scientific achievement, was given to George Cotzias, certain members of the Lasker committee resigned in protest. Shortly afterward the American Association for Research in Nervous and Mental Diseases made a special award to Oleh Hornykiewicz, citing the same achievement.

Today Hornykiewicz reflects on the ill feelings that arose between Cotzias and the other scientists who had earlier tested levodopa as a treatment for Parkinson's: "Cotzias made a specific and important contribution. He showed that large doses given orally and chronically produced excellent results. He simply went far beyond what we would have thought possible with dosages of dopa. He did not see any effect with lower doses, so he kept going up, up, and up. That is, I think, the American approach to things, including medicine."

The last time Hornykiewicz met Cotzias was at a symposium in New York in 1975. "Cotzias didn't mention any controversies anymore. We talked to each other like normal people. I was very glad about that..."

Cotzias spent the last months of his life doing research on the effects of levodopa on cancer. He died of that same disease in 1977 at the age of 58. Andre Barbeau died in 1986, age 54, following a number of heart attacks. He never forgave Cotzias.

The first levodopa preparations were not very efficient. After passing through the stomach into the small intestine, the early, simple form of medication made its way through the bowel wall and into the bloodstream. From there it traveled around in the body, much of it being converted to dopamine before it reached the brain. This process might take hours, and the end result was that only about 10 percent of the dose reached the brain. A solution to the problem was found by combining levodopa with a substance that inhibited the metabolism of levodopa in the periphery of the body and until the drug could reach the brain.

In the United Kingdom carbidopa was used as the inhibiting substance and the resultant tablet carried the trade name Sinemet. In continental Europe benserazide was used as the inhibitor, and the trade name for the levodopa tablet was Madopar.

However it is dispensed, levodopa is truly a wonder drug. By substituting for the missing dopamine in the brain, levodopa mitigates symptoms and gives victims of Parkinson's an extended lease on life.

When first administered, levodopa is effective in about 75 percent of cases. It is a safe drug: in the first few years of levodopa treatment only two deaths were attributed to its use. Both were a result of striking improvement in the well-being of Parkinson's patients. One patient cut down a tree and the other played a set of tennis. After completing their exertions, both patients died suddenly.

But levodopa works for only so long. There is a diminishing therapeutic effect. After a period of between three and six years, the inexorable progress of Parkinson's disease demands higher and higher doses of levodopa, which causes increasing side effects sometimes as severe as depression and delirium.

And even during the period that it is effective, levodopa has its shortcomings. Often there is "end-of-dose" akinesia in which there is a gradual return of symptoms three or four hours after taking the pill. More troublesome, and much more embarrassing, are "on-off" phenomena, characterized by unexpected loss of mobility, with sudden freezing of posture.

Levodopa is not a cure. Nor does it slow the progress of Parkinson's disease. Symptoms are relieved, but the underlying pathological cause of the disease — the decay of dopamine-producing cells in the substantia nigra — continues as before.

When doctors went in search of a adjunctive drug — one that would prolong the efficacy of levodopa, reduce the need for increasingly higher dosages, blunt the side effects — they found one in deprenyl. Over time deprenyl became established as a helpmate to levodopa in the middle and late stages of Parkinson's disease. It was not known by what means deprenyl played this beneficial role. Nor was it suspected for some time afterward that deprenyl might have a protective effect on the dying cells that give rise to the symptoms of Parkinson's disease. Furthermore, no one imagined deprenyl might become the *first drug ever to slow the progress of neurodegenerative disease.*

6

THE EARLY YEARS OF DEPRENYL

FOR MANY YEARS AFTER IT WAS FIRST synthesized in a laboratory in Budapest, deprenyl lead a precarious existence. It was conceived in 1960 as a "me too" drug, meant to be the Hungarian version of a successful American drug used in the treatment of high blood pressure. It was all but abandoned at its birth until, afterward, it was suggested that it might be useful in relieving depression, hence the name deprenyl. It did, indeed, prove to be an effective antidepressant in clinical trials on soldiers in Soviet hospitals, but deprenyl's career seemed finished in 1963. In that year doctors learned that monoamine oxidase (MAO) inhibitors could cause liver damage, sometimes resulting in death.

Deprenyl was a member of the outlaw family of drugs called MAO inhibitors.

For the next several years MAO inhibitors, which had been one of the most popular of antidepressants, were used only when doctors could carefully monitor patients' diets to guard against the eruption of side effects. The easier way was to use alternative antidepressant medications. MAO inhibitors went out of style. They lost their commercial appeal, and doctors were not interested in hearing about a new version.

There is some dispute about who had the original idea for deprenyl. But the question may be moot: it is nothing short of serendipitous when a drug is designed to attack a particular problem in the body and turns out to accomplish just that objective. More frequently a molecule becomes a therapeutic drug when it is discovered, post hoc, that the molecule just happens to have some desirable consequence within the organism.[1] What that consequence may be is highly speculative. And there may turn out to be more than one consequence. Phenylbarbital, for example, may be used as an antianxiety agent, an anticonvulsant, or a hypnotic. Much of the creativity in the development of new drugs, then, comes not from designing a seemingly suitable molecule in the laboratory, but from observing the unpredictable effects that molecule may have when it is introduced into the body.

Deprenyl, it was thought, might be useful in the treatment of high blood pressure or hypertension because it was modeled on pargyline, an antihypertensive drug developed by Abbott Laboratories, a U.S. pharmaceutical company. The chemical properties of a drug are sometimes predictive of its pharmacologic effect. That is, a molecule similar in structure to par-

---

[1] A molecule becomes a drug only after it is registered with the World Health Organization. Deprenyl was the original name registered with WHO; although the international nonproprietary name has now been changed to the chemical designation, selegiline hydrochloride, the drug is still known "in the literature" as deprenyl.

gyline might be expected to have an antihypertensive result. If that expectation is met, then the "me too" molecule may be patented as a new drug.

This is the way most drugs are developed. They are variations on a theme. For a pharmaceutical company to proceed otherwise — to begin experimenting with an entirely new molecular structure called a *de novo* molecule — is far too unpredictable, too risky, and too expensive.

It is another tenet of the pharmaceutical industry that the potential success of a new drug may be measured in some rough proportion according to the "popularity" of the disease it is intended to treat. In the 1950s one of the most "popular" diseases was hypertension.

Being hypertensive is popularly supposed to mean being high-strung, emotional, or nervous, but, in fact, it describes a condition in which a person's blood pressure is higher than average for his or her age. The cause or causes of hypertension are largely unknown — hence the term *essential hypertension* — but what is known is that it is a condition that may lead to strokes, heart attacks, kidney failure, and other dysfunctions. Overall, it might be said that hypertension leads to more deaths than any other disease.

Not many years ago people diagnosed as being hypertensive were told that the only way to ameliorate their condition was to get lots of rest and to eat well-balanced diets, avoiding red meats and reducing salt intake. Occasionally there was a resort to surgery: by cutting nerve fibers from the spinal cord, doctors were able to cause the blood vessels to dilate. In the 1950s drugs were introduced into the treatment of hypertension. One of these classes of drugs, diuretics, caused the kidney to excrete salt and water, thus lowering the amount of fluid in the body and decreasing blood pressure. Another type of drug, vasodilators, act directly on the walls of the blood vessels to enlarge them.

Most of the other drugs used to treat hypertension were targeted at the brain. MAO inhibitors were among them.

To the powers-that-be at Chinoin Pharmaceutical and Chemical Works, Ltd., in Budapest, it seemed that a remedy for hypertension would find a ready market. Chinoin had a storied history and had been associated with the development of a number of important new drugs. But these were few and far between. Despite the special care and support afforded by the Government to the Hungarian pharmaceutical industry, Chinoin was too reliant on the sale of low-priced generic ingredients. The knowledge and resourcefulness of the company's hundreds of research chemists were curbed and stifled by its isolation from world markets.

Like so many pharmaceutical companies, Chinoin had been an outgrowth of the paint and dye industries. It was founded in 1910 by the son of a paint store owner, Emil Wolf, who was sent to Berlin to study chemistry so that he could understand the composition of enamels and paints. When Wolf returned to Budapest, he became interested in chemical synthesis rather than producing materials derived from plants and animals. In 1913 he synthesized a new derivative of quinine, which he called chinoin, and thereafter that was the company's name.

Almost all of Chinoin's early products were sold under license from Bayer, the German pharmaceutical giant. International recognition as a drug company in its own right came in 1937 when one of Chinoin's consultant professors, Dr. Albert Szent-Györgyi, was awarded the Nobel prize for the development of ascorbic acid or Vitamin C.

In 1948 Chinoin was nationalized, and two years later the Hungarian government took measures to promote and intensify drug research. The three largest pharmaceutical companies, Chinoin, Gedeon Richter, and EGYT, were given new laboratories, and to support their efforts the government established a Drug Research Institute with 170 of its own chemists.

For Chinoin especially there was another important relationship. Beginning in the 1930s a close cooperation developed with Semmelweis University whereby the school's department of pharmacology would test the compounds synthesized by Chinoin and, on occasion, would suggest to Chinoin's chemists an idea for a chemical entity that might have some biological potential. Joseph Knoll, when he became head of the department of pharmacology in 1961, nurtured this symbiotic relationship.

The hundreds of chemists at Chinoin experimented over and over again in the quest for a chemical entity or molecule that might turn out to be the right size, shape, and fit to modify the body's chemistry in a desired way. As a pharmacologist, Knoll was less interested in the architecture of a drug than in its effects on the living organism.

The present-day headquarters of Chinoin Pharmaceuticals and Chemical Works is a seven-story building, clad in blue aluminum, in Ujpest, a busy manufacturing district of Budapest. The offices are decorated in the 1950s utilitarian style of glass and formica.

The buildings at 5 To Utca comprise one of three

major production sites owned by Chinoin. It is the most important, responsible for the research and development of synthetic and biosynthetic pharmaceuticals. At another plant on the outskirts of Budapest, Chinoin produces pesticides and other plant protective agents, and near the northern Hungary town of Miskolc, a new plant manufactures and packages injection products.

Chinoin enjoys certain distinctions in Hungary. It was the first Hungrian company to enter into a foreign production agreement following inauguration of the New Economic Mechanism in 1968 by Prime Minister Janos Kadar. That was a bold step.

The pesent managing director of Chinoin, Istvan Bihari, says that at the end of Kadar's economic experiment, which lasted five years, "the leaders of the reform were put a little bit aside. Not executed, not hanged, not imprisoned, which is a very important thing if you take history into consideration." Bihari is a clever man with an impish sense of humor. He became the head of Chinoin in 1982 when Hungary was beginning once again to look to the West as a market for exports and a source of foreign capital.

In the summer of 1989 Chinoin was grooming itself for the capitalist procedure of selling shares to the public. The Hungarian government had enacted new legislation to attract foreign investors, and the long-defunct Budapest Stock Exchange was about to be reopened.

Chinoin was getting ready to turn its best face to a larger public. The company is a potentially fertile source of drug technology: of its 4,300 employees, almost 1,000 are engaged in research and development. If all other things were equal, Chinoin would have an important economic advantage over pharmaceutical companies in the West: in 1988 the average salary of its scientists was the equivalent of $2,600.

But Bihari is also well aware that, for a pharmaceutical company, international recognition depends very much on the discovery and development of new drugs. It was important to Chinoin that the company be identified with deprenyl. Bihari acknowledges the important role played by Knoll in the development of deprenyl, but adds, "Every drug has more than one parent. Chinoin is the mother of deprenyl."

Deprenyl originated and was first synthesized in the laboratories of Chinoin. There is equally no doubt that deprenyl would not have survived if not for the tenacity and persistence of Joseph Knoll.

All drugs produce more than one effect. The primary effect is the desired therapeutic effect. In addition, there are always "secondary" effects, or side effects, either because a drug causes multiple reactions within the same organ or because it also causes reactions in some other organ or organs of the body. The ideal would be a drug that traveled directly to the targeted area of the body, there to perform its therapeutic work. But there are always side effects. Sometimes these are pleasant and harmless. When they are unpleasant, or harmful, scientists call the offending drug "dirty." The more organs in the body that are receptive to a particular type of drug, the greater the chances the drug will have "dirty" consequences.

It was one of Knoll's accomplishments to show that deprenyl, unlike all the other MAO inhibitors then on the market, was highly specific and selective. The drug concentrated its action where it was supposed to — on the brain. There were side effects, as with all drugs, but they were not serious, nor were they harmful.

Mood-altering drugs were all the rage in the 1950s and early 1960s, and MAO inhibitors were the first true antidepressants. They deserved to be called wonder drugs: they were also used as antihypertensive agents, and occasionally, they were prescribed to relieve angina pectoris, a chest pain caused by inadequate blood flow.

It was first as an antihypertensive, modeled on pargyline, and then as an antidepressant, that deprenyl worked its way through the development process at Chinoin. The chemist under whose supervision the drug was developed was a Chinoin employee named Zoltan Eczeri. Born in 1927, Eczeri joined Chinoin upon graduation as a chemical engineer in 1950 and quickly rose to become head of the research laboratory. The pharmacologist who tested the drug was Joseph Knoll.

Eczeri and Knoll shared an interest in drugs that affected the central nervous system. It followed that both were also interested in the effects of amphetamine.

Perhaps more than any other substance amphetamine has kept alive the faint hope that a drug can improve human performance. According to one comprehensive review of scientific literature, "Amphetamine seems to hasten conditioning, to restore, in part, the degraded rate at which a new discrimination is learned by sleepy subjects, and to increase the rate at which subjects acquire proficiency in a motor skill." There is no evidence to show that these effects are permanent — nothing to show that amphetamine improves physical or intellectual performance except in a temporary way.

At Chinoin it was decided to build a molecule that combined an amphetamine derivative, methamphetamine, with a pargyl chemical group used in the synthesis of pargyline. The pargyl group was known to confer antidepressant activity, and it was thought that the addition of methamphetamine, because of its mild stimulatory activity, might produce a better MAO inhibitor.

Amphetamine had fist been used as a central stimulant in 1935 to treat narcolepsy, an affliction characterized by fits of sleep and sleepiness. Although amphetamines are still used to treat a variety of diseases, their efficacy depends on strict control of dosages.

Knoll says that the idea for deprenyl came to him in 1960 when he was intrigued by the discovery that amphetamine in low doses helped rats to maneuver around stationary objects. In large doses, almost predictably, it had the opposite effect. When he analyzed the effect of amphetamine on rat brains, he deduced that low dosages of the drug acted *selectively* but that high dosages had a number of other effects, some of them undesirable.

Knoll says that this finding prompted him to search for a new derivative of amphetamine that would have only a selective effect on the brain. That drug turned out to be deprenyl.

Elizabeth Miller remembers only that she was assigned to design a molecule based on pargyline. Miller was a laboratory technician at Chinoin, freshly graduated as a chemical engineer. She remembers that it was the habit of her boss, Zoltan Eczeri, to scour the latest scientific journals for reports and descriptions of new drugs. When he read about a new drug that had become a commercial success, he would assign to one of his chemists the task of "me tooing" the structure of the drug.

Eczeri suggested to Miller that pargyline had a "good structure." It was an active drug, meaning that it made something happen when it entered the body, and it was susceptible to chemical modification that might improve its biological effect. Miller spent two years building a molecule that combined the pargyl chemical group with methamphetamine. Working by herself, she synthesized 250 variations of a molecule, recording the procedure of each synthesis in pencil in a brown, lined notebook. The final molecule was designated E-250.

Elizabeth Miller turned 55 in 1989. She lives in a tidy yellow bungalow with her husband, Miklos, a mechanical engineer, and two daughters who are both physicians. She is a pretty woman, soft-spoken, and paralyzed from the waist down by muscular dystrophy.

Miller speaks very quietly. "Eczeri was a nice man, very intelligent. It is very difficult to remember, because it is so long ago. Dr. Ezceri was a frequent visitor to the library. He read there, and he would come back and say, 'I have a very good idea.' It was a time when pharmaceutical work was without any organization. We did not have the base of information that has been made available by modern computers. It was very much trial and error. Dr. Eczeri was like our research department — he would decide what we would do, and we would try it.[2]

"So Dr. Eczeri suggested that I make this compound based on pargyline. Dr. Knoll investigated it and found

---

[2]Eczeri died of cancer in 1985 at the age of 56.

the compound to be very good. After that he [Knoll] suggested that it be used in clinical studies, for instance in the Soviet Union. And it was a very good antidepressant — it had very good activity."

The first patent for deprenyl was issued on December 13, 1962. According to custom, it carried the names of the people associated with the development of the drug in proportion to their contribution. Patent number 151090 cited four names:

Zoltan Eczeri	32.5 percent
Elizabeth Miller	32.5 percent
Joseph Knoll	25 percent
Eva Somfai	10 percent

(Eva Somfai was the patent lawyer.)

E-250 was only one of a number of drug compounds under development at Chinoin, but it was clearly regarded as an important one. It was the company's attempt to build a better MAO inhibitor, and because MAO inhibitors had found such a wide market as antidepressants, E-250, if successful, could turn out to be an important product.

By 1964 Knoll and Eczeri had conducted enough tests, using rats, to be satisfied that they had succeeded in combining the MAO inhibition characteristic of pargyline with the stimulant effect of amphetamine. The first scientific paper about deprenyl appeared in the *Archives of International Pharmacodynamics* and was entitled "Phenylisopropylmethylpropinylamine (E-250): A New Spectrum Psychic Energizer." The authors, Knoll and Eczeri, concluded: "E-250 proved to be a potent psychic energizer of broad spectrum of action, which acts both as an acute psychostimulant and a chronic psychic energizer in animal experiments, but unlike amphetamine, it does not increase motility significantly and lowers blood pressure."

"E-250: A New Spectrum Psychic Energizer" was the first time that Knoll had published in the English language.

Just as deprenyl was given its name, and clinical trials on humans were beginning in the Soviet Union, MAO inhibitors went out of favor. A growing number of cases of liver damage suggested that this class of drugs was not only inhibiting enzymes in the brain, but also in the body's busiest center of metabolism — the liver. MAO inhibitors were effectively preventing the oxidation of dopamine and other neurotransmitters in the brain, thereby relieving symptoms of depression, but they were also preventing oxidation of another type of amine called tyramine.

When the action of the enzyme monoamine oxidase is inhibited in the liver, the metabolism of tyramine is blockaded. Instead of being transformed into an inert chemical, tyramine finds its way into the bloodstream where it may cause hypertension.

Tyramine is particularly abundant in aged cheese. It is also present in other dietary foods, including broad beans, yeast extracts, chicken liver, pickled herring, chocolate, red wines, and even beer. A combination of a MAO inhibitor with any food containing high amounts of tyramine could result in hypertensive symptoms, including painful neck stiffness, nausea, severe headache, and palpitation. Worse, hypertensive crises had on rare occasions resulted in hemorrhage, strokes, or cardiac failure.

The collection of side effects caused by MAO inhibitors became known as the "cheese effect."[3] MAO inhibitors were taken off the market and were later used only with strict dietary controls. Deprenyl had not yet reached the market, however. It was still only an experimental drug. But deprenyl was an inhibitor of the enzyme monoamine oxidase, and didn't MAO inhibitors cause the cheese effect? A disappointed Chinoin put its new drug on the shelf.

Significant research, though, was being conducted elsewhere. In 1968 a chemist working for a British pharmaceutical firm conducted a series of experiments that led to the synthesis of a compound called clorgyline. The chemist, whose name was J. P. Johnston, found to his surprise that clorgyline did not inhibit all monoamine oxidase. It tended to concentrate its action on cells outside the central nervous system and it seemed to inhibit only the monoamine oxidase that occurred outside the brain.

Johnston decided there must be two types of monoamine oxidase. He designated them MAO "A" and MAO "B." His clorgyline inhibited the type "A" that occurred in the body's periphery, including the liver.

One question remained: was there a substance that inhibited the "B" type of monoamine oxidase that occurred primarily in the brain?

Joseph Knoll made his first appearance before an audience of Western scientists in 1971 at a conference in Sardinia held in honor of Oxford University's

---

[3]During the years that MAO inhibitors were withdrawn from use, the *Journal of the American Medical Association* found some black humor in the cheese effect, quoting the lines: "a tiny bit of camembert!/What strange illusions linger there/What visions direful and distressed/Through hours that should be sweet with rest."

Herman Blaschko, the dopamine man and mentor of Oleh Hornykiewicz, who had argued for so many years that dopamine was an important constituent of the body.

Knoll was not unknown among his peers, although being from behind the Iron Curtain, he was regarded as something of an oddity. At this conference — the subject was monoamines — it was an occasion for him to be asked to make a presentation.

Knoll's paper was entitled "Some Puzzling Pharmacological Effects of Monoamine Oxidase Inhibitors." He reviewed the results of the once-popular MAO inhibitors, pointing out that all of these drugs, "to date," had been seen to exert multiple effects on the body. One of these effects, the cheese effect, could be potentiated by the ingestion of even a small amount of cheese containing only a few milligrams of tyramine.

Knoll had conducted simple animals tests, using cats and rats, to ascertain the effects on tyramine of four MAO inhibitors. The first three MAO inhibitors had been widely used in the treatment of depression. All "potentiated" the harmful effects of tyramine. The fourth, deprenyl, a new and experimental substance, behaved in a different manner. Deprenyl was the first MAO inhibitor to be shown to "antagonize" the harmful effects of tyramine.'

While clorgyline inhibited the MAO enzyme classified as "A," deprenyl seemed to inhibit only the "B" enzyme — the one whose destructive activity was centered in the brain.

Knoll had proven that deprenyl had the most important quality sought in any drug: it was "selective." Deprenyl discouraged the action of monoamine oxidase and supported the maintenance of dopamine in the brain. Elsewhere in the body, unlike all other MAO inhibitors, it behaved in an innocuous fashion. It caused no damage to the liver.

Yet the world was not ready to believe someone like Knoll. His "proof" came from experiments with rats and cats. Humans might be different. There might be "species differences."

Knoll also knew that whatever evidence he might present would be either suspect or ignored if it came from behind the Iron Curtain. To prove deprenyl's selectivity would require the testimony of scientists from the Western world.

7

THE "DISCOVERY" OF DEPRENYL

DR. WALTER BIRKMAYER is a towering figure in the treatment of Parkinson's disease. He became famous after Oleh Hornykiewicz asked him in 1961 to test levodopa on Parkinson's victims. Thereafter, his name became linked to the discovery of the first rational drug treatment for the disease. His office in Vienna became the shrine for Parkinson's victims. His patients came from throughout Central Europe. His bedside manner gave rise to the term *Birkmayer effect* to describe his seemingly extraterrestrial healing powers.

Birkmayer is an old man now, in his ninth decade. He is a physician, not a scientist, who was educated long before biochemistry and physiology were brought together with other disciplines to form the study of psychopharmacology — the effect of drugs on the brain. His trial-and-error method is sometimes smiled at by his peers, who say he does not practice the scientific method. Yet he has made some of the most important discoveries in the treatment of Parkinson's disease.

It was Birkmayer, for example, who was among the first to use a decarboxylase inhibitor with levodopa. Everyone expected the result would be to prevent the "levodopa response" in the brain. They were wrong and Birkmayer was right: the inhibitor preserved the levodopa from degradation until it could be transported through the bloodstream through the brain.

It was Birkmayer who decided to try deprenyl in the treatment of Parkinson's disease.

In 1974 there was little prospect of deprenyl ever becoming a commercial drug. Knoll had argued before the group of scientists at Sardinia in 1971 that deprenyl did not potentiate the harmful side effects known collectively as the cheese effect, but deprenyl was a MAO inhibitor, and it was fixed in the minds of doctors everywhere that these enzymes were responsible for the cheese effect and therefore should not be prescribed.

Sometime in November 1974 Dr. Moussa Youdim, an Iranian, suggested to Walter Birkmayer that he might want to experiment with deprenyl on his Parkinson's patients. The concept of using a MAO inhibitor to treat victims of Parkinson's was not new: Birkmayer himself, during his earlier relationship with Hornykiewicz, had shown that MAO inhibitors appeared to discourage the breakdown of dopamine in the brain. But those MAO inhibitors caused the cheese effect. There was no point in carrying on with such experiments.

Maybe deprenyl was different, Youdim suggested to Birkmayer. Over a period of seven months Birkmayer administered deprenyl to 44 Parkinson's patients, hoping to measure the drug's potential abilities to relieve the akinesia that is characteristic of the disease.

"The results," Birkmayer noted, "Were remarkable in the 'off' periods [when patients were in their most immobile state]. Thirty minutes after intravenous injections the patients were able to walk, and the performance of all their movements was improved."

While the most dramatic effect followed intravenous injection, the improvement after oral medication lasted twice as long. Even patients in the earlier stages of the disease, who were not yet suffering from immobile periods, showed improvement.

According to an article summarizing these findings and written by Birkmayer and Youdim, "At present we cannot say how long the duration of the improvement will last. Up till now this is an experience with deprenyl of only seven months . . . We are also unable to answer the question whether in long-term treatment deprenyl will have any beneficial effects." There was no mention in the article, nor in the acknowledgments or references, of Joseph Knoll.

The results of Birkmayer's first trial with deprenyl were preliminary and short-term. They were reported in 1976 in the *Journal of Neural Transmission*, a German publication of limited circulation. Deprenyl, in its new guise as a treatment for Parkinson's disease and not just an antidepressant, attracted little notice.

Two years later Birkmayer and Youdim were ready to report the results of a long-term trial using deprenyl and involving many more patients. Equally as important to the future of the drug, a group of scientists in the United Kingdom were preparing to prove once and for all that deprenyl was a MAO inhibitor that did not cause the cheese effect.

115

The article that opened the door to the worldwide use of deprenyl appeared in *The Lancet*.[1] Again the authors were Birkmayer and Youdim, along with two other clinicians. By this time Birkmayer was able to report the long-term effects of deprenyl combined with levodopa.

This larger study was based on the experience of 223 elderly patients, almost equally divided among those who had had the disease for seven years or less and those who had been Parkinson's victims from seven to fifteen years. The doctors measured the disability for each patient according to ten variables: gait, pushing, jumping, speech, writing, associated movements, posture, mimicry, start, and self-care.

Six months after the patients had deprenyl added to their levodopa regimen, the improvement in their disability was more than 50 percent in the group that had been parkinsonian for up to seven years and more than 60 percent in the group that had had the disease for more than seven years. Less than 15 percent of the patients failed to show any response to deprenyl, and there was no significant incidence of side effects. This improvement was maintained for a further 21 months, which Birkmayer and Youdim believed demonstrated that deprenyl acts immediately and has a sustained therapeutic effect over long periods.

With the article in *The Lancet*, a highly respected and widely read medical journal, Birkmayer and Youdim announced that deprenyl was a new, effective treatment for Parkinson's disease.

It was an unseaonably warm day in the spring of

---

[1]"Implications of Combined Treatment with 'Madopar' and Deprenyl in Parkinson's Disease: A Long-Term Study," *The Lancet* (1.439.1977).

1977, but Merton Sandler had good reason to keep his overcoat on as he passed through customs at London's Heathrow air terminal. Each pocket of his coat concealed one and a half kilograms of a white crystalline powder. Sandler, a medical doctor and honorary consultant chemical pathologist at Queen Charlotte Maternity Hospital, was not used to this sort of thing. He felt a sense of relief when he found himself outside in the fresh air.

Before the drive home to Twickenham, Sandler called his friend and colleague Gerald Stern, who was a consultant neurologist at University College Hospital. The contraband white powder was the chemical compound deprenyl.

Although Sandler and Stern had long known each other, their careers had converged only in the 1970s. Sandler's research interest had always concerned the role of monoamines in metabolizing foods and all other chemicals that enter the body. Stern's interest was disorders of the central nervous system, most particularly Parkinson's disease.[2] The two men began to work together when it was recognized that drugs that inhibit the action of monamine oxidases might have a role in the treatment of Parkinson's disease.

In 1971 Sandler and Stern learned about a MAO inhibitor that, unlike its cousins, might not have a poisonous effect on the liver. It was, as Sandler remembers, the first time Knoll had presented a scientific paper in the non-Communist world. Although Knoll had previously published dozens of scientific articles,

---

[2]In 1982 Stern and Andrew Lees, consultant neurologist at the National Hospital for Nervous Disease, University College and Whittington Hospital, wrote *Parkinson's Disease: The Facts* (Oxford University Press, 1982), the most readable and comprehensive layman's explanation of Parkinson's in all its aspects.

none had yet appeared in English. "At the time," Sandler recalled in the summer of 1988, "we didn't think it was anything special. It was nice to meet him. You know, a proper scientist from behind the Iron Curtain. There weren't too many drugs emerging from behind the Iron Curtain. It's pretty Third World, and it still is, with certain exceptions I now know, like Knoll, who does fantastic work."

In his paper Knoll had argued that a MAO inhibitor, which he called deprenyl, did not, in contrast to other MAO inhibitors, cause the cheese effect.

Sandler and Stern became further interested in deprenyl when they learned the drug was being used on an experimental basis by Dr. Walter Birkmayer. A controversial man with no training in biochemistry, Birkmayer was, nevertheless, a shrewd clinician, and his keen observations attracted the attention of every doctor and scientist interested in Parkinson's disease. Birkmayer's experiments, and his sometimes exaggerated claims of success, prompted Stern and Sandler to smuggle deprenyl into the United Kingdom and to conduct their own tests on human patients. They contacted Knoll, who was pleased to oblige.

Merton Sandler's office is a tiny, book-lined room on the second floor of the pathology building at the rear of Queen Charlotte Maternity Hospital. From there he leads a research team of 20 scientists of several nationalities. The thread that connects all of this research is monoamine metabolism. The dominating interest is the role of monoamines in neuropsychiatric disorders. Sandler is a warm, engaging man who takes almost a schoolboy relish in recalling how he acted as a courier in the smuggling of deprenyl a dozen years ago. "They didn't check me as I was leaving Hungary, thank goodness. At Heathrow I just brazenly walked through. Can you imagine doing that today with the kind of security they have at airports now?"

Gerald Stern is a reserved man, distinguished in deportment as well as dress. In a small loft at Middlesex Hospital in the West End of London, Stern explained how he and Sandler and a few of their colleagues went about conducting tests of deprenyl.

"First, we took it [deprenyl] ourselves to be sure it was safe. Then we had to obtain permission to give it to patients. But it was a different ball game at that time. We had to write to what was called the United Kingdom Medicines Commission. We explained what we'd done and where we got the drug from and so forth, and we wanted the Commission to allow us to use the drug with patients. There was a long delay. We couldn't get a reply out of them, and we were becoming increasingly frustrated because we thought we had our chins out in front of others, if only for a few milliseconds. And I kept ringing up the Medicines Commission, and they were holding meetings to discuss it, and then there was a final meeting . . . and they wouldn't give a decision.

"And I said to them, 'Well, can you explain to me the difficulty?'

"And they said, 'Well, it's like this. We are a bureaucracy and we have regulations. And we have stated regulations for drugs that are invented in this country, and we have regulations for drugs that are manufactured outside the United Kingdom and imported here. But we have no regulations for drugs that are *smuggled* into the United Kingdom. Therefore we cannot render a decision.'

"And I said, 'What do we do? We've got a drug that seems to be safe.'

"And they gave us a lovely reply. They said, 'You realize you musn't quote us on this, but you must understand the Commission cannot give you its permission to use this drug. But would you please let us know the results in due course!'"[3]

In 1977 Stern was, at the age of 47, the recognized authority in Great Britain in the study and treatment of Parkinson's disease. At that time his attention was centered on the baffling nature of the "on-off" oscillations, the abrupt and often unpredictable changes in the mobility of Parkinson's patients who were given the standard levodopa therapy. On-off oscillations made it all the more difficult for Parkinson's sufferers to plan their lives: the threat of sudden immobility was enough to discourage people from leaving their homes. "In half of our patients," Stern says, "successful control of the symptoms was beginning to deteriorate in a way we couldn't understand. We were looking desperately for some other form of treatment, and it was claimed, by Birkmayer, that deprenyl could provide better control of symptoms."

But deprenyl was a MAO inhibitor, and before using the drug, Stern had to satisfy himself that it did not potentiate the cheese effect. Knoll had shown this to be the case in laboratory experiments with animals; it re-

---

[3]Government control of drugs in England and Europe, unlike the USA, is limited virtually to toxicity because new uses for a drug are discovered as doctors observe its effects. Deprenyl, for example, began as a drug for high blood pressure. It was later used for depression. It was only after years of usage that deprenyl was recognized as a miracle drug capable of protecting the brain's vital dopaminergic system — a discovery that would never have been made if medicine in England and Europe was controlled by regulations similar to those of the FDA in the United States.

mained to be demonstrated that deprenyl was a special MAO inhibitor that did not cause hypertensive crises in humans.

In London 10 persons were found who agreed to be the first humans deliberately exposed to the combination of a MAO inhibitor and tyramine, which causes the cheese effect. Four of the human guinea pigs were "normal" males; six had Parkinson's disease (four males aged 38-62 years, and two females aged 71 and 72 years). The University College Hospital and Medical School Committee on the Ethics of Clinical Investigations gave approval for the tests, which were to be conducted in hospital and with full resuscitative measures available in case of a hypertensive reaction.

Over a period of two months the test group was to be given 10 milligrams daily of deprenyl. Each week the volunteers were put to bed and given progressively doubled doses of tyramine at 30- to 45-minute intervals until either an agreed maximum dose had been reached or until there was a pronounced slowing of heart rate or rise in blood pressure. The maximum amounts of tyramine were far higher than those likely to be encountered in a normal diet.

The four "normal" volunteers were able to tolerate relatively large doses of tyramine after they began taking deprenyl. All reported "feelings of well-being, increased energy, and light-headedness" during the deprenyl treatment. The six patients with Parkinson's disease had a lower tolerance for tyramine before the deprenyl treatment, but after taking deprenyl their response was similar to that of the "normal" volunteers. In fact, "no decrease in tyramine tolerance occurred in four of the [Parkinson's] patients after two months of deprenyl therapy at a dose of 10 milligrams daily."

The inference from these results was that "substantial amounts of tyramine, considerably larger than those likely to be encountered in a diet containing even the most generous quantities of cheese, could be eaten with impunity" by people taking moderate doses of deprenyl, by then categorized as a "B" type monoamine inhibitor. This was in sharp contrast to the results of other tests using an "A" type monoamine inhibitor, where only small amounts of tyramine were sufficient to provoke a profoundly disturbing response.

Stern, Sandler, and colleagues concluded: "The claim of Knoll that deprenyl administration is free from the cheese effect has now received substantial experimental backing and the drug may thus find important applications in clinical practice." Their paper, published in 1978, was the first to show that deprenyl was a special kind of MAO inhibitor that did not have the cheese effect.[4] What Joseph Knoll had shown to be the case with his experiments on cats, Stern and Sandler demonstrated to be true in humans. And Gerald Stern had found a drug that could be used to control the symptoms of Parkinson's disease and also to moderate the side effects of levodopa, including the on-off oscillations, which themselves were often so similar to the symptoms of Parkinson's. Even after deprenyl was shown to be without the cheese effect, every major pharmaceutical company in Western Europe turned down the opportunity to market the drug. The reasons for this lack of interest are to be found somewhere in

---

[4]Elsworth, J. D., Glover, Vivette, Reynolds, G. P., Sandler, M., Lees, A. J., Phuapradit, P., Shaw, K. M., Stern, G. M., and Kumar, Parveen, *Deprenyl Administration in Man: A Selective Monoamine Oxidase B Inhibitor without the "Cheese Effect"* (*Psychopharmacology*, 1978).

the economics of the pharmaceutical industry. Every new drug is measured by pharmaceutical companies according to some risk-reward ratio, and the prospective reward from deprenyl, whose potential around 1980 seemed to be only as an adjunct in the treatment of late-stage Parkinson's disease, was not sufficient to arrest the attention of a major drug firm. Merton Sandler comments wryly: "Or at least that's the way it seemed to their financial analysts at the time."

The manufacturer of deprenyl, Chinoin Chemical and Pharmaceutical Works, assigned European rights to Farmos Group Limited of Helsinki. Finland was the trade gateway from the Communist world to Western Europe, and Farmos seemed to Chinoin the best staging platform from which to launch the drug in the West. In the end, the United Kingdom license ended up with the Finnish Sugar corporation, whose business in the United Kingdom was conducted through a company called Forum Holdings.

The headquarters of Forum Holdings is a modern red brick building on the main street of Redhill, a small town in Surrey, 40 minutes by train from London. Forum is the parent company for a group of U.K. subsidiaries that deal in sugar and in a range of products that contain sugar, such as Evening Primrose Oil. By 1982 the vagaries of the sugar market led Forum Holdings to consider a program of diversification. Accordingly, in September 1982, Forum incorporated a new subsidiary, Britannia Pharmaceuticals Limited, to be the license holder for deprenyl in the United Kingdom. Days later, on October 1, 1982, the drug became available on prescription in Britain.

By 1988 Britannia's sales of deprenyl had risen exponentially to the point where the drug was the single biggest product distributed by Forum Holdings or any of its subsidiaries. Through pharmaceutical wholesalers, who distribute the drug to pharmacists and hospitals, Britannia sold 60,000 packages of deprenyl, each containing 100 tablets, bringing aggregate revenues of 2.8 million pounds sterling. These numbers may be interpolated to suggest that deprenyl was being used by 15,000 persons in the United Kingdom, or 25 percent of all Parkinson's patients undergoing levodopa treatment.

The Parkinson's Disease society of the United Kingdom (PDSUK) was founded in 1969 in the bedroom of Mari Jenkins, whose sister Sarah was a victim of Parkinson's. Jenkins was a formidable woman: when she died in 1989, she was eulogized in obituaries in the *Times*, the *Daily Telegraph*, the *Guardian*, and elsewhere in the media.

Today, at an office at 36 Portland Place, a few steps from the headquarters of the British Broadcasting Corporation, the Parkinson's Disease Society is under the enthusiastic stewardship of Anthony Kilmister.

"From a tiny organization Kilmister says, "PDSUK has grown to a very large one, with 160 local chapters in cities and towns all over the United Kingdom. Our income is now two million pounds per annum, whereas when I took over in 1972 it was probably 20,000 pounds. And all that money is from private donations. It is not government funding. It is all raised from the public through special events, galas, and legacies. A lot of people leave us money in their wills."

PDSUK helped to finance much of the research work conducted by Stern and Sandler and their colleagues following the important clinical trial that showed deprenyl did not cause the cheese effect. With some pride, Kilmister says, "We were way ahead of North America."

In the United Kingdom the privileged relationship between doctors and patients is more formally observed than in North America, and therefore the success of the drug in therapeutic terms is more difficult to measure. The management of Britannia Pharmaceuticals cites evidence that deprenyl is increasingly being used to smooth out the fluctuations in symptoms associated with levodopa therapy. Tony Kilmister of PDSUK refuses to identify people who are taking deprenyl, but he says, "I think it's enabled people who've had difficulties . . . deprenyl has really revolutionized their lives. Not for everybody, but in a large number of instances it's helped people enormously by getting them back onto a stable plane. I have come across people who've really been able to carry on when, prior to taking deprenyl, life was really getting really grim — when they were running out of steam."

The two neurologists in the United Kingdom perhaps best qualified to assess the effects of deprenyl are Gerald Stern and Andrew Lees. In 1982 their book *Parkinson's Disease: The Facts* spoke optimistically of the prospective therapeutic effects of deprenyl:

> Deprenyl possesses the extraordinary quality of selectivity, blocking only the enzyme which destroys dopamine and allowing the normal degradation of other monoamines to continue. Deprenyl is therefore free of . . . restricting "cheese effects" yet it is able to increase brain dopamine by preventing its nor-

mal breakdown within nerve cells and in the gaps between the nerve fibers. As a result it can be used safely with L-dopa or any of its combinations and dietary restrictions are unnecessary. When given alone, deprenyl has only slight effects on the disabilities of Parkinson's disease, but it can enhance the action of small doses of L-dopa. More importantly, in patients experiencing a wearing-off effect from each dose of L-dopa, the addition of deprenyl may prolong the duration of benefit. It [deprenyl] has the advantage that it is easy to use ... and its unwanted effects are singularly few.

Seven years after their book was published, Stern and Lees had time to reflect on the properties of deprenyl, its use in the treatment of Parkinson's disease, and the possibility that it might affect the pathological aging process of humans in general.

Lees had been Stern's protégé, but by 1989 he had become, in the words of Tony Kilmister, "quite a young chap in his own right and a name to be conjured with." Lees's well-trimmed beard does not disguise his youthfulness. He is 40 and runs the movement disorder clinic at University College Hospital as well as being consultant neurologist at the National Hospital for Nervous Diseases in London's Queen's Square. His long, brisk strides suggest he is a busy person in a hurry. His reputation is that of a cautious scientist who awaits proof before committing his opinions.

"You know," Lees says, "that we had it [deprenyl] very early. We got it in 1977, and we had five or six years extensive experience in using it here before it was really available, even on an experimental basis, in the United States. We found it to be a useful drug for patients who were losing ground on conventional levodopa therapy — that it was something you added in when they were beginning to 'drop off the end,' as it were. And we were also quite impressed by its effects on sharpening people up in a rather nonspecific way and its undoubted alerting effects, making people feel better, whether or not it improves their motor disabilities. And it has an interesting role in improving attention . . . But certainly, anecdotally, a number of European investigators have been struck by that additional effect the drug has."

8

THE HUNGARIAN CONNECTION

THE MAN WHO BROUGHT DEPRENYL to North America is that rare blend of businessman and scientist. Don Buyske looks like neither. He is tall and rugged and looks and dresses like a forest ranger, which he once was. But he is a true scientist, with a fondness for hypotheses. He likes to try things out. "You tell me if I'm full of crap. And I'll tell you if you're full of crap. You know?"

Dr. Donald A. Buyske is a gregarious man, which is one of the reasons he found himself hunting boar near Budapest in 1971. At the time, Buyske was vice president of research and development at the world's most diversified health care company, Warner Lambert, and he had been invited by a friend of a friend to investigate the possibility of some kind of relationship between Warner Lambert and certain companies in the Hungarian pharmaceutical industry. It was during that visit that Buyske first heard the name deprenyl, but he did not pay much attention. He was more interested in getting access to all of the drugs and all of the drug technology that Hungary had to offer.

Buyske's interest in matters Hungarian was long-standing. Anyone whose career is in the field of bio-chemistry can hardly avoid Hungarians, and Buyske's first close encounters with Magyar scientists had occurred following the Budapest revolt in 1956, when he was the youngest ever director of research at Ayerst Laboratories, a division of American Home Products, in Montreal. Since then he had heard all of the jokes — "a Hungarian is someone who follows you into re-volving doors and comes out ahead of you" — but he has his own jokes, too, which are a kind of purple tes-timony to the tenacity and accomplishment of the Hungarian people. After Ayerst Laboratories, there were a lot of reasons why Buyske became, in the U.S. pharmaceutical industry, the Hungarian Connection.

His ancestry was not one of them, however. Buyske was born into a Polish Catholic family and grew up with his three sisters and two brothers in a suburb of Milwaukee. He followed his father, a career officer with the U.S. Justice Department, to Tucson, Arizona, where he attended elementary school, and to Spring-field, Missouri, where he limped along in secondary school and spent his spare time collecting bottles of water, for reasons that are obscure in his memory, and rocks. Buyske now believes this interest in water and rocks was a subliminal expression of his interest in science. He says that the sharp, clear, single event that changed the course of his life was winning the top marks in a high school science exam.

"That gave me some recognition, some visibility. All of a sudden I discovered, whoopee, that I had some talent. I was taken under the wing of two wonderful teachers, two spinsters — one in physics, one in chemistry. I became kind of their pet. That's what egged me on. That's how it happened. After that, it never crossed my mind that I would ever be anything but a chemist."

As it turned out, he became not a chemist but a bio-chemist. At the end of World War II the United States awakened to biochemistry. Of course, there had been previous research in the U.S. into the chemical re-actions of the body and how they maintained life. But the history of biochemistry had been written by scien-tists with distinctly European-sounding names, begin-ning in the early nineteenth century with Friedrich Wohler, who first synthesized an organic compound from inorganic material. Well into the twentieth cen-tury, the honors in biochemistry went to men with German names, such as Otto Loewi, who shared the 1936 Nobel prize for his work demonstrating that nerves transmitted impulses by chemical means.

The founder of chemotherapy, the use of chemical substances to treat disease, was Paul Ehrlich, another German. Ehrlich, who died in 1915, made the first suggestion that drugs interact with chemical group-ings, which he called "receptors," in the body. This notion that chemical interactions in the body had to do with the physical structure of molecules gave rise to hopes that drugs could be designed by logical thought and calculation. Such was not to be the case. The busi-ness of discovering new therapeutic drugs continued to depend on an understanding of the nature of dis-ease, on luck and opportunity, and on the experience and intuition of researchers.

Biochemistry, then, was an art as well as a science, somewhere on the border between biology, the study of living things, and organic chemistry, the study of the composition and properties of living things. In the years following World War II the United States embraced biochemistry, and thereafter the discovery of new drugs settled into an Anglo-American orbit.

Buyske discovered biochemistry during his summers as a forest ranger in Montana. Watching for fires from atop lookout towers he whiled away the hours reading about Wohler, Ehrlich, and Loewi. He loved it.

Buyske earned a degree in chemistry in 1949 at Springfield College in Missouri. He was a chemist. At graduate school at the University of Wisconsin, he needed three more credits to complete his Ph.D. "And my professor said, 'Why don't you take a course in biochemistry?' So I took a course in biochemistry. My eyes were opened to the linkage between organic chemistry and life. I was in love. Elated."

Those were the years when the early attempts were being made to understand the mechanism of action of vitamins, the nutrients that are essential for growth and metabolism. Buyske remembers, too, the excitement about the development of new antibiotics. It was the golden age of pharmaceuticals.

Buyske's first job was measuring the oxygen content of sewage, working in a nutrition laboratory where his task was to observe the effects of different foods on chickens. He was tempted by offers from several pharmaceutical companies, but along came a fellowship from Duke University in North Carolina. Teaching was "pure pleasure," but by now he was married, and after two years he departed academe to join private industry. He became a member of the research staff of Lederle Laboratories, which is in New York State and, for a young scientist, close to the excitement of New York City.

In New York Buyske was instrumental in founding a discussion group the met periodically at the Academy of Sciences. These ad hoc gatherings would discuss new concepts, new discoveries, new drugs. The conversation frequently turned to psychotropic drugs — drugs that affect mood and that were now widely used in the treatment of psychiatric disorders. They also talked about the effects of these new psychiatric drugs on the catecholamines, the chemical messengers of the brain. Buyske remembers that it was at one of these meetings, an informal get-together over beer and cheese, that he first met Joseph Knoll.

"And one of the things we talked about then was: what's going on in the brain with these neurotransmitters?" Buyske could not have known how importantly Knoll and a particular neurotransmitter called dopamine would loom in his future.

By now Buyske was in his mid-thirties, an impatient age. He uprooted his family and moved to Montreal to direct the research department of Ayerst Laboratories. It was his introduction to the new and varied culture of Canada's predominantly French speaking province of Quebec. The chemists and pharmacologists at Ayerst were a polyglot bunch, from Germany, Italy, and other Western European countries. At Ayerst Buyske was also introduced to a large contingent of Hungarian scientists, many of whom had left their homeland during or as a result of the 1956 revolt.

After a four-year sojourn in Montreal, Buyske moved to New Jersey, now as vice president for scientific and medical affairs at Warner Lambert. The products of his new company included not only prescription drugs, but also a bewildering range of health care and consumer products, including chewing gum, shaving cream, razor blades, and mouthwash.

Two things about Warner Lambert appealed to Buyske. One was the company's plan to increase spending on the development of new drugs. The second was its intention to expand the scope of its international operations. Buyske's penchant for reading scientific papers, and his exposure to the cosmopolitan group of scientists at Ayerst in Montreal, had convinced him there were molecular compounds around the world waiting to be turned into therapeutically useful and commercially profitable drugs.

Within two years of his arrival at Warner Lambert, Buyske was hunting wild boar in Hungary. His companions were Don O'Neill, marketing vice president at Warner Lambert, Dr. Edward Goldberg of Chicago, and their host, Dr. Richard Burget.

In the summer of 1970 Eddie Goldberg had been invited to Budapest to work on a blood product called Bioplast developed in Hungary. Goldberg is a professor of experimental surgery at Michael Reese Hospital and Medical Center at the University of Chicago. He had long been interested in new products that aid physicians in artery repair or in blood replacement using synthetic or hemoglobin-modified products. The person who invited Goldberg to Budapest was Richard Burget.

It is impossible to trace the hierarchy in Hungary, then a Communist country, but there is no doubt that Burget, who is a private citizen, is a man of considerable influence. Through Burget, Goldberg became familiar with the four pillars of Hungary's pharmaceutical industry — three companies called Chinoin,

Gedeon Richter, and EGYT, and a fourth entity called the Institute for Pharmaceutical Research. To Goldberg, all of them seemed to be bursting with white-coated researchers whose test tubes and Bunsen burners were filled with ideas for new pharmaceuticals. His suggestion that there might be a market for Hungarian drug technology in the United States met with enthusiastic response.

On his return to Chicago, Goldberg telephoned his friend Don O'Neill, whose company, Warner Lambert, had an international perspective. The question was: would the company be interested in a deal with the Hungarians? O'Neill introduced Goldberg to his colleague, Don Buyske, Warner Lambert's expert in scientific and medical affairs, and Buyske prepared to make the first of what would be many visits to Budapest. Subsequently, over the next two years, there were efforts to mediate an agreement between Warner Lambert and the Hungarian drug industry.

Buyske became the point man on these visits, not because he was a marketing expert — that was O'Neill's role — but because he was an expert at recognizing the potential of new drugs. He had heard of a Hungarian drug called deprenyl because he knew all about MAO inhibitors. He had "read the literature" and was familiar with their use in the treatment of depression. To him, deprenyl was another of those MAO inhibitors. "It didn't get entrenched in my mind that deprenyl was really quite different. I was aware that the drug had some special properties but, you know, being intellectually honest with myself, I just thought that deprenyl was kind of interesting. Nothing more."

His interest was in negotiating the rights to all of the pharmaceutical products that came out of Hungary, and he proposed just such a deal on behalf of Warner Lambert. Long negotiations followed. Buyske's patience was thoroughly taxed by the lumbering bureaucracy of Hungary's state-controlled trading company. "And then all of a sudden a god-damned lawyer, one of our guys, walks in and says it's his absolute duty to protect Warner Lambert from guys like me who want to do something different. Finally, out of sheer exhaustion, both parties walked away. We would have had a deal, it was in the typing stage. I blame it on the lawyers."

For Buyske, not all was lost. He had established close relationships in Budapest, and he renewed his acquaintanceship with Joseph Knoll. Then it was back to Morristown, New Jersey, the head office of Warner Lambert, and the day-to-day business of directing research and monitoring drug developments at other companies and in other countries. There he met another Hungarian, an expatriate named Laszlo Darko.

One of Buyske's responsibilities at Warner Lambert was the supervision of the clinical testing of new drugs. In 1971, his own medical staff fully occupied, he dispatched a new prescription product for testing to an independent company in New York. Clinical Research, Inc., was in the business of designing the procedure, or protocol, of clinical trials, arranging to have the studies done in three or four different medical centers, analyzing the data, and preparing a detailed final report. The young man assigned to carry out this assignment was Laszlo Darko.

In 1956 at 10:00 p.m., November 26, Darko had gone AWOL from the Hungarian army, slipping across the Austrian border and surrendering to the U.S. Army at Salzburg. Wearing a new pair of shoes and carrying

1,000 Austrian schillings, both donated by the Red Cross, Darko was transported to the United States and billeted with an expatriate Hungarian family over the Christmas holidays. It is a measure of Darko's resourcefulness that, within a month, he was able to improve his English enough to win a scholarship to a small college in New York State.

Darko was good at winning scholarships. He pursued postgraduate studies at two Midwestern universities and then spent several years apprenticing with a major international pharmaceutical firm. His tenure at Clinical Research in New York was short, but it was important to his future. It was there that, as a "monitor" of clinical drug studies, he learned the practicalities, politics, and personalities of making new drug applications to the Food and Drug Administration. By the mid-1970s Darko was allowed to return to Hungary, and he did so on a frequent basis. He made the rounds of the pharmaceutical companies and universities, including the Semmelweis University School of Medicine, and brought back to the United States processes for new over-the-counter drugs. Warner Lambert, with its large nonprescription drug business, seemed a likely customer, and Darko came knocking on the door of the vice president of scientific and medical affairs, Don Buyske.

During one such visit, Darko offered Buyske a new antacid that was under development in Hungary. It was better than Warner Lambert's Rolaids and Gelusil because it had longer-lasting effects, but Buyske was unable to sell the preparation to his colleagues. On another occasion Darko turned up with a horseradish extract that was supposed to restore or stimulate hair growth. This product never reached the U.S. market.

Neither did an anti-acne lotion that Darko offered to Buyske. But the relationship between Buyske and Darko had found common ground — their mutual interest in drug technology from Hungary.

Hungary had seldom been out of Buyske's mind since his first visit to Budapest. He had become a founder of the U.S. Hungarian Trade Council. And there were other little things that cemented his relationship with the Hungarians. One of these was his role, however minor, in returning the Crown of St. Stephen to Hungary.

In Hungary the Crown of St. Stephen is more than just a piece of regalia. In Hungarian tradition the three elements of the nation are the Crown, the people, and the land. The Crown is a symbol of Hungarian national pride. In the closing days of World War II, while Soviet armies laid siege to Budapest, the Crown left the city in a mysterious special train and was hidden in Austria. Eventually it fell into the hands of the Americans, who locked it up in Fort Knox. Although the Communist government on several occasions demanded its return to Hungarian soil, it remained in the U.S. until the 1970s.

In 1981 Buyske's life underwent some profound changes. He was divorced from his wife, and he divorced himself from Warner Lambert to join Johnson & Johnson, another widely diversified pharmaceutical company. At J&J his title was vice president for business development, international, and it gave him all the more scope for reading scientific papers and traveling the world in search of new products, a task in which Laszlo Darko was retained as a consultant.

Darko, like Buyske, was aware of deprenyl. At that time — 1981 — no U.S. Pharmaceutical company was interested in the drug. It would not be easy to win approval to sell deprenyl in the United States: the FDA would never accept the results of clinical and other studies conducted in Europe; the worldwide patent was due to expire in three years, after which any company could copycat the drug; and the U.S. market for the drug was thought to be too small for any company to take on the development, registration, and premarketing costs. "In the U.S.," Buyske says, "deprenyl was a dead issue."

It seems strange in light of later events that deprenyl in the early 1980s had so little prospect of joining the approved pharmacopoeia of drugs in the United States. Deprenyl had now been used for varying periods of up to a dozen years in a number of countries in Europe and South America. It had a record, abroad, of tens of thousands of patient-years without serious adverse incident. Walter Birkmayer and other clinicians had proven that the drug had therapeutic value: it improved the well-being and the outlook for people with Parkinson's disease. Yet the prognosis for deprenyl in America in the early 1980s was bleak.

How can a drug with the potential to improve and perhaps extend lives be denied to the people of a continent that has the world's most advanced health care? The answers, in the case of deprenyl, are multifarious, but center around the FDA's control of medicine.

To begin with, it would be a mistake to assume that a drug with demonstrated therapeutic value is automatically added to the armamentarium of treatments available to physicians. A very large gap exists between the available scientific information on drugs and their uses in medical practice. A pharmacologist may determine that a drug appears to have a desired effect on human tissue and a clinician may show that the drug has a beneficial effect in humans, but there are a number of further steps before physicians may be persuaded to prescribe the drug. These steps involve not only regulatory authorities, but also the pharmaceutical companies that build the bridge of information to physicians.

But the pharmaceutical companies must first of all decide whether it is worthwhile to market a new drug. There are isolated cases to the contrary, but generally speaking a pharmaceutical company will not produce a drug, no matter what its merits, unless the size of the potential market for that drug is sufficient to yield a return on their investment that they might stay in business.

Deprenyl did not meet that criterion. Since higher standards of testing had been imposed by the FDA in 1962 the cost of introducing a new drug in the United States had risen to more than $100 million. Only four percent of new drugs could be expected to reach sales of $50 million a year, and less successful drugs required 10 years or more to recoup their development costs. Deprenyl, even if it were in that category, could not wait that long: its worldwide patent would expire in 1984.

And deprenyl was still a minor drug. It was not even a *primary* therapy. It was an adjunctive drug to levodopa treatment, its official use was limited to patients in the middle and late stages of Parkinson's disease. This translated into a potential market in the United States of little more than 25,000 patients, and perhaps 2,000 to 3,000 in Canada. A market of this size would hardly entice a pharmaceutical company to invest tens of millions of dollars to obtain FDA approval.

There was also the incidental fact that deprenyl's mechanism of action was not fully understood. Medical knowledge of "why" is not a prerequisite for the use of a drug — the reasons for using aspirin in the treatment of arthritis are entirely empirical. And deprenyl came with a reputation. It was a MAO inhibitor, and in the minds of many doctors, all MAO inhibitors carried the clear connotation of dangerous toxicity — the cheese effect.

In 1982 the North American rights to deprenyl resided with Farmacon, Inc., a private company owned by the indefatigable Laszlo Darko. The rights had been "parked" with Darko, along with some additional drug technology owned by Chinoin Chemical and Pharmaceutical Works, on the understanding that he would serve as a broker to find a company that would take on the development and marketing of deprenyl in the United States. In spite of his tenacity — even in Budapest Darko was described as the type of Hungarian who tried to climb in the window after he was thrown out the front door — he had been unable to sell any part of this package, including, of course, deprenyl.

At Johnson & Johnson, his new employer, Buyske's mandate was to investigate new prescription products abroad. This suited him. He traveled frequently to Europe, and his visits to Japan totaled more than 50. He was on the editorial board of one scientific society, active in four others, and was a consultant to the U.S. government.

Buyske knew as much as it was possible for one person to know about the development of new drugs around the world. He had published 60 papers on the chemistry, pharmacology, and biochemistry of new

drugs. He himself had introduced, or helped to introduce, several new products, including four anti-
infective drugs, two topical steroids, a tranquilizer,
and an antidepressant. In all, he was responsible for
the introduction of 10 new drugs into the U.S. market,
not to mention the first consumer self-test for preg-
nancy.

He had another important asset: he had attracted a
wide circle of friends in the scientific community. They
were to become important to him in persuading the
Food and Drug Administration that deprenyl was a
safe, worthwhile product. But that was in the future.

Meanwhile, Buyske was approached by represen-
tatives of S. C. Johnson & Son, Inc., the world's largest
manufacturer of consumer and industrial wax products and one of the biggest family-owned corporations
in the United States.

Johnson Wax is an unusual company. Founded in
1886, it dominates the city of Racine, Wisconsin, where
its streamlined headquarters, designed by Frank Lloyd
Wright, have been described as "not only the greatest
piece of twentieth-century architecture realized in the
United States but also, possibly, the most profound
work of art that America has ever produced."[1] Johnson
Wax is known for its paternalism: it was among the
first U.S. corporations to introduce paid vacations,
shortened work weeks, and an employee profit-
sharing plan. Throughout its history the company
prospered because of its enlightened relations with
employees and its merchandising savvy. But it is less
renowned for its scientific research.

---

[1]Kenneth Frampton, introduction to *Frank Lloyd Wright and the Johnson Wax
Buildings* by Jonathan Lipman (New York: Rizzoli, 1986).

In 1981 the current patriarch, Samuel Johnson III, was interested in diversification and made plans to enter the proprietary health care business, an activity that includes nonprescription or "over-the-counter" drugs. Buyske was charmed by Sam Johnson and by the company, but he was not thrilled at becoming an apothecary. "When they called me, I said, 'No, no way! I'm not interested in toilet bowl cleaners and furniture polishes. I'm an R_x guy! I'm a high-tech guy!'"

Money overcame Buyske's strategy to keep Johnson Wax at bay. "Finally, I told them, 'You can't afford me.' And they said, 'You name it.' So I said, 'Four hundred and fifty grand.' I figured I'd never hear from them again. Well, son of a gun if that's what they didn't offer me. Who the heck would pay a nut like me $450,000? But they did."

He was now embarked on a new chapter of his peripatetic career. "I took the research staff and I shook 'em. A thousand people, give or take, and I got rid of a third of them because they were incompetent. In a nice way, because Johnson Wax is a very generous company. They had guys in the lab who 20 years before were frying hamburgers at White Tower, somehow got into the lab as a dishwasher, and then became a researcher. That was okay when you were just mixing a little glup here and a little glup there and you were calling it Pledge or some damn thing. But those days were gone. They didn't know any science. They didn't have a technical base. They had one small laboratory computer — would you believe this! I'm talking about 1981!"

With the arrival of Buyske, the sacramental headquarters of family-owned Johnson Wax was to become the gateway to North America for Hungarian pharmaceuticals. The business of prescription drugs was a far cry from the manufacture of wax products and pesticides, but Sam Johnson was willing to take the leap. His great-grandfather, Samuel the first, would have been proud.

The founder of S. C. Johnson & Son knew about diversification: 100 years before, he had begun to sell wax as a way of promoting his parquet flooring business. The North American practice of scrubbing floors with strong soap and hot water made preservation of the little wooden blocks known as parquetry difficult. The first Sam Johnson investigated the European custom of protecting floors with waxes, and before long he was selling more wax than flooring. Now Samuel Johnson III was about to draw again on European technology, albeit from a farther remove, since Hungary was behind the Iron Curtain.

But prescription drugs were still some distance in the future. To buy a pharmaceutical company would be prohibitively expensive, even for Sam Johnson, and it would be almost as expensive to start from scratch with the development of ethical drugs. The over-the-counter business was the next best thing.

At Johnson Wax Buyske set about building a proprietary health care business. His new colleague was Dan Rogers, a former president of Revlon, Inc., and a man whose talents lay in marketing. Together they decided to attack the consumer franchise of Metamusil, a highly successful product manufactured by Monsanto. Metamusil, a mild laxative, is composed of psyllium seed and dextrose. Buyske was aware of the public ambivalence toward sugar, a feeling that ran deep among people who were health conscious. So he proposed replacing the dextrose in Metamusil's formula with a fiber substance. Rogers hit upon the name Fiberal and Johnson Wax had its first major entry in the over-the-counter health care market.[2]

All during this time, though, Buyske stayed attuned to the changes in Hungary. He was familiar with the managers of Chinoin, and he knew the potential possessed by the company's hundreds of research chemists. The portents were improving for a commercial agreement between a U.S. company and a Hungarian company. For one thing, the Communist country's state trading apparatus for the pharmaceutical industry, Medimplex, had yielded its monopoly on foreign agreements, and Chinoin, along with other drug companies, was free to pursue its own deals abroad. Chinoin yearned for the foreign capital that only an American company could provide, and Buyske was eager to get back into the business of prescription drugs. Both were aware that entry into the U.S. market, the most lucrative of all, would be made so much easier through the introduction of a "name" drug. With such a prestige drug, Buyske might be able to persuade Sam Johnson to vault into the prescription drug business.

In 1982 research into Parkinson's disease was near a dead end. No cause could be found, and therefore a cure was every bit as elusive. And then, in California, a group of heroin addicts began to exhibit symptoms of parkinsonism. They were too young to have the most common form of the disease. Their disorder was induced by a drug — a synthetic heroin transformed in the brain into a poison that destroys the cells in the

---

[2]Buyske's product concept for Fiberal was later copied by five other companies, including the manufacturer of Metamusil.

substantia nigra. Deprenyl was shown to prevent the poisonous action of this drug.

In Washington the U.S. Congress passed the Orphan Drug Act to give special patent protection to new drugs used in the treatment of rare diseases. Don Buyske persuaded the FDA that deprenyl could qualify as an orphan drug. And in Vienna Walter Birkmayer announced that deprenyl increased the life expectancy of Parkinson's patients by as much as two years. Now deprenyl had a real chance to be approved by the FDA.

9

MAKING THE CASE FOR DEPRENYL

✦ BARRY KIDSTON DEVELOPED THE SYMPTOMS of Parkinson's disease shortly after he bought himself a chemistry set in the summer of 1976. Kidston was in his early twenties, too young to have Parkinson's disease, or at least the type that develops slowly and insidiously over most of a lifetime and then manifests itself with immobilizing symptoms in later years. Yet he did have Parkinson's; the difference in his case was that the disease developed suddenly and the symptoms struck quickly.

Although it was not realized for some time, the tragedy of Barry Kidston provided an important clue to the unknown cause of Parkinson's disease. The most prevalent theory about the cause or "aetiology" was that it was a contaminant somewhere in the environment. That environmental poison could be anything — in the food we eat, in the air we breathe. Before Barry Kidston, the task of tracking down that poison seemed impossible because the usual type of idiopathic Parkinson's disease takes root many years before its victims become aware of the symptoms. The responsible contaminant — if indeed the cause was in the environment — might be something we were exposed to in childhood or adolescence. It could be anything.

What Barry Kidston offered to researchers was an unusual model of Parkinson's disease. In his case, there appeared to be a singular, identifiable cause of the disease. It was somewhere in that chemistry set. And the poison, whatever it was, had the unusual property of traveling straight to the dopamine-producing neurons in the brain's substantia nigra. This was the very site of the damage that took so many years to develop in most sufferers from Parkinson's. Kidston presented a case of almost instant parkinsonism. Once the poison was discovered, scientists could use it to induce the syndrome in all manner of animals, and they would have reproducible animal models for studying the disease.

Those who study human disease like to have what they call good animal models in order to follow the progress of the disease and to test treatments that might be therapeutic in human patients. The poison that made Barry Kidston parkinsonian might be expected to do the same to rats, cats, dogs, and monkeys.

Kidston was an American student addicted to hard drugs. With his new chemistry set, he began making narcotics in the basement of his parents' home. One model he chose was Demerol, a powerful painkiller that provides a high not unlike that induced by heroin. Demerol was relatively simple to copy, and Kidston, by manufacturing a molecule of similar structure, could make a drug that looked the same, tasted the same, and had the same effects. Probably through haste he eventually produced a bad batch. By using too much heat, he inadvertently made a drug called MPTP. When he injected the MPTP, his body froze and he became mute and tremulous.

In light of his history of psychiatric disturbances, Kidston was at first diagnosed as a catatonic schizophrenic and treated with electric shock. Later, because his symptoms were so similar to parkinsonism, he was given levodopa therapy, which gave him relief. It was as if this young man had Parkinson's disease.

MPTP was a drug that had been developed 30 years before and had been tried experimentally by a number of pharmaceutical companies in the treatment of several disorders, including heart disease and hypertension. One company abandoned clinical trials after two patients died. Others were suspicious that the drug might be highly toxic. It was not the practice to make public the results of these experiments. MPTP was just another substance that was the subject of routine pharmacological tests.

In 1978 Barry Kidston sat under a tree, took an overdose of cocaine, and died. An autopsy showed that there was an absence of black pigment in his substantia nigra — the sign of advanced cell decay. That proved that Kidston did indeed have Parkinson's disease at the age of 24.

Kidston's name, however, did not become famous until some years later. Although seven scientists prepared an article detailing the circumstances of his drug habit and death, the article was rejected by the *New England Journal of Medicine* and the *Journal of the American Medical Association*. Finally it appeared in a new and much less prominent scientific journal, *Psychiatry Today*, published in Holland. It attracted little notice.

There had been other cases of MPTP poisoning, but they had either not been properly diagnosed or had not come to public attention. A chemist in New Jersey — at age 37 an unlikely candidate for Parkinson's disease — had found, after working with MPTP, that his coordination was lost. Another chemist in Denmark had spent nine years in a psychiatric ward after similar exposure in the laboratory to MPTP. Both, as it turned out, had become victims of Parkinson's disease.

What MPTP needed in order to become recognized was an engine of publicity, and it found one in the person of Dr. J. William Langston, a young clinical neurologist in San Jose County, California. Langston had no basic research experience, but he was very articulate, lent an attractive face to television cameras, and didn't hesitate to inform the media of his discoveries. He made MPTP famous. At the same time he also helped to make deprenyl widely known in North America.

It started in July 1982 when Langston treated a prisoner in a local California jail who seemed to have symptoms of Parkinson's disease. The prisoner was in a frozen state, as was the prisoner's girlfriend. The only thing they had in common was that they were heroin addicts.[1]

Within weeks of convening a press conference to report this strange phenomenon, Langston had found several young addicts in Northern California who had developed symptoms of parkinsonism after injecting a synthetic heroin. One of a number of "designer drugs" manufactured in underground laboratories in the

---

[1] A filmed documentary of Langston's unraveling of the MPTP mystery was telecast in Great Britain and the United States and was entitled *The Frozen Addict*.

United States, the synthetic heroin was contaminated with MPTP.

MPTP became the focus of worldwide research into Parkinson's disease. The chemical had a peculiar affinity for the brain's substantia nigra — it left other organs in the body undamaged — and it soon proved to be a valuable tool. In animal tests, for example, MPTP showed that parkinsonism symptoms did not begin to appear until there was a loss of more than 80 percent of the cells in the substantia nigra. This fact confirmed the suspicion that the disease is the result of a long, slow process of degeneration of the dopaminergic cells.

MPTP is not itself a poison; the damage to the substantia nigra cells is caused instead by a by-product of MPTP called MPP+. When MPTP passes from the bloodstream into the brain, it is converted by an enzyme into the much more poisonous compound MPP+. To stop this conversion process is to neutralize MPTP.

The enzyme responsible for the conversion of MPTP into the poisonous MPP+ is monoamine oxidase B. MAO B is the same enzyme that eats up dopamine, and deprenyl inhibits the activity of MAO B.

Langston, as well as doctors and scientists elsewhere, became very interested in deprenyl. If the real cause of Parkinson's disease is some kind of external contaminant, like MPTP for example, and since deprenyl blocks the damaging effects of MPTP, would not deprenyl similarly interrupt the action of other poisons that might reach the substantia nigra? Furthermore, would not deprenyl halt or slow down Parkinson's disease in its early stages?

The renewed interest in Parkinson's disease in general and in deprenyl in particular gave a new perspective to Don Buyske's plans to make a deal with Chinoin Pharmaceutical and Chemical Works. Buyske thought, if Johnson Wax could begin with a pharmacy of products, such as those that might be available under license from Chinoin and perhaps the other Hungarian drug companies, and there was a prestige drug somewhere in the package they could be successful. Deprenyl was starting to look like it might be such a prestige drug.

But deprenyl, even if someone were willing to foot the bill, still faced the FDA approval process in the United States, not to mention all the costs of FDA mandated testing for efficacy and side effects, as well as the expense of preclinical development and safety and clinical evaluations. Deprenyl had a record in Europe of 150 thousand patient-years of experience without serious adverse incident, but it was problematical how far the FDA would go in accepting the results of experience outside the U.S.

Would deprenyl be treated by the FDA as an "NCE" — a new chemical entity? Or would the FDA make some allowances for all the testing and experience outside the U.S.?

The Orphan Drug Act, enacted by the U.S. Congress in 1983, made it possible for Buyske to pursue government approval for deprenyl. The act recognized that the pharmaceutical industry would not sponsor extensive research for drugs with a small market, so it provided incentives for research and marketing of drugs used to treat rare disease. More than 5,000 disorders are considered rare, including Huntington's disease, Tourette syndrome, and muscular dystrophy, and most rare diseases affect fewer than 50,000 people in the United States.

What was most appealing to Buyske about the new legislation was the provision that a drug designated as an orphan would be granted exclusive marketing rights in the United States for seven years. This was an essential safeguard: deprenyl's worldwide patent, registered by Chinoin in 1964, would expire in 1984. If deprenyl proved to be a commercial success, the lack of a patent would open the way to duplication of the drug by rival companies. The Orphan Drug Act would obviate that problem in the U.S.; it would protect deprenyl from competition for seven years.

In the new act, Buyske saw the opportunity to persuade the FDA that deprenyl, if approved, would be prescribed to only a relatively small population of patients in the United States. For Sam Johnson the rights to Hungarian drug technology provided the basis upon which to diversify from the proprietary drug business into prescription drugs.

In the end, it took nine months for Johnson Wax and Chinoin to negotiate the license agreement that granted Johnson Wax the western hemisphere rights to all of Chinoin's pharmaceutical preparations and technology.

Six months later an application to approve the sale of deprenyl by Johnson Wax was made to the FDA. The application included all of the clinical, chemical, and toxicology data that had supported the approval of the drug in the United Kingdom in 1982. Nevertheless, the response from the FDA was negative. The regulatory agency suggested that approval, if it were ever granted, would take a long time.

The FDA said that the application to approve deprenyl: (a) did not provide sufficient evidence of the safety and efficacy in patients with Parkinson's disease and (b) did not provide the results of preclinical tests normally required for the assessment of potential toxicity and other risks.

In short, the FDA wanted more information and concluded by stating that the file was closed. "If you wish to reopen it, the submission should be in the form of an amendment to this application, adequately organized, which represents the information necessary to remove all deficiencies we have outlined."

Deficiencies? Tens of thousands of people in England and Europe had used deprenyl for over 10 years. It had a medical record of over 150,000 patient-years without adverse incident. All empirical evidence was dismissed by the FDA without evaluation as though it did not exist. The sick be damned.

Sam Johnson could see a long road ahead before the FDA could be persuaded to approve deprenyl. In the meantime he became aware of a flaw in the Orphan Drug Act. Despite all of the incentives in the act, there was no protection against product liability law. Johnson Wax could be sued for design defect, failure to warn, and negligence in testing.

In the early 1980s juries in product liability cases were awarding progressively greater damages in cases of personal injury or death. Liability insurance premiums were going through the roof, and Sam Johnson cold see that if his company were to be sued because of a new pharmaceutical product, his birthright might be at stake. He decided to remove his new prescription drug business from the orbit of Johnson Wax. The cost to produce prescription drugs was just too high.

In January 1986 a new company was incorporated to acquire the prescription pharmaceutical business of S.

C. Johnson & Son, Inc. Its name was Somerset Pharmaceuticals, Inc., and its largest shareholders were, as well as Johnson Wax, two Wall Street venture capital companies. The chairman and chief scientific officer became Dr. Donald A. Buyske. However, though Buyske had the title of boss, he was a minority shareholder.

Deprenyl was beginning to acquire a mystique. Its use in the treatment of Parkinson's disease was well established in Europe. The MPTP story opened up the possibility that deprenyl might be useful as more than an adjunctive drug and might even slow down the progress of Parkinson's. And now the drug was being tested in a number of other disorders of the central nervous system.

The brain is not composed of discrete compartments; it is an organ of interdependent parts. The question arose whether deprenyl, by improving the "tone" of the dopaminergic system, might not be useful in treating other neurodegenerative diseases.

Alzheimer's disease, for example, seemed to be the result of brain damage in regions removed from the dopaminergic system. Yet some scientists were contemplating trials with deprenyl on victims of Alzheimer's. There might not have seemed to be any scientific reason to use deprenyl other than that it sometimes worked as an overall tonic.

All along, Walter Birkmayer had continued to experiment with deprenyl. By 1983 he had prescribed the drug to hundreds of patients over a period of almost nine years. When he sat down to analyze the results, he found a startling fact. Those patients who had taken deprenyl as an adjuvant drug to the convention levodopa therapy had lived for a considerably longer

155

period of time. Did this mean that deprenyl, by blocking the activity of the MAO enzyme in the brain, slowed the progression of Parkinson's disease?

Slowing the progression of a degenerative disease would itself tend to prolong life. Birkmayer was tempted to make the further inference that deprenyl, through some unexplained psychostimulant effect caused by the release of more dopamine, increased life expectancy. A deficiency of the neurotransmitter dopamine in the brain was known to be the culprit in Parkinson's disease, but Birkmayer was prepared to grasp the hypothesis that the health of the dopaminergic system was more broadly related to the aging process.

The results of Birkmayer's analysis were published in 1985 in the *Journal of Neural Transmission,* a European scientific publication.[2] The title of the paper was "Increased Life Expectancy Resulting from Addition of L-Deprenyl to Madopar Treatment in Parkinson's Disease: A Long-Term Study." Among Birkmayer's five co-authors were Joseph Knoll and Moussa Youdim, the Iranian clinician who had introduced Birkmayer to deprenyl.

The choice of the phrase *increased life expectancy* was provocative. Many drugs allow people to live longer by providing relief from the symptoms of disease or, less commonly, by providing a cure. What became known as "the Madopar study" suggested that deprenyl not only had the effect of prolonging life, but of increasing life expectancy. There is a big difference.

---

[2]"Increased Life Expectancy Resulting from Addition of L-Deprenyl to Madopar Treatment in Parkinson's Disease: A Long-Term Study," Birkmayer, W., Knoll, J., Riederer, P., Youdim, M. B. H., Hars, Vera, and Marton, J., in *Journal of Neural Transmission*, Vol. 64 113-27 (Springer-Verlag, 1985).

The Madopar study was not long in attracting attention or controversy. The conclusions of the study were attacked because they were based on a retrospective analysis — i.e., Birkmayer had not embarked on the study with a view to demonstrating that deprenyl increased life expectancy. His objective, when he began the study in 1974, had been to measure the efficacy of deprenyl in mitigating the side effects of Madopar, the trade name for a combination of levodopa and a carbidopa substance that helps levodopa to reach the brain.

At the end of nine years Birkmayer compared the results in 377 cases of patients who had received Madopar alone, and 564 cases of patients who had taken deprenyl as well as Madopar. The Birkmayer study covered the period from 1976 to August 1983. Of the 941 patients whose progress he monitored, 81 were taking both Madopar and deprenyl at the inception of the study. Others began to take deprenyl as the effects of Madopar alone began to wear off. The average time the 564 of the total 941 patients took deprenyl was slightly less than four years.

The starting point for the survival analysis was the date that each of the patients began to be treated with Madopar. At the conclusion of the study in 1983 the survival analysis was based only on that group of patients who had died (the others, of course, having an indeterminate future life). What Birkmayer found was that those patients who had taken deprenyl during the nine-year period lived an average 15.3 months longer than those who had not.

As in all such long-term studies embracing a large sample of people, there were dropouts along the way. The number of dropouts in the Madopar group was roughly proportionate to the number of dropouts who had been on a combined Madopar-deprenyl regimen. If the dropout group had been included in his data, Birkmayer discovered, "the difference in survival is even longer — 28.6 months — in favor of the deprenyl-treated patients."

The controversy surrounding the Madopar study was stoked by Birkmayer's methods, personality, and background. No one could dispute his talents as a doctor. Parkinson's victims came to his office in Vienna from all over Europe. Such was his empathy with his patients that the term *Birkmayer effect* became popular as a way of describing his extraordinary powers of healing. But Birkmayer did not have the affection of all his peers.

Behind a wrought-iron gate at Schwartzpanier-strasse 15 in the hospital district of Vienna, one of the plaques reads:

UNIV. PROF.
Dr. Walter Birkmayer
NERVENARZT

One flight up broad stone stairs on the door to his office, there is a gold engraving of Birkmayer's likeness. Inside, in the waiting room, is a large oil paint of Birkmayer flanked by scrolls for various awards he has won for his work in medicine. Dr. Birkmayer is not a man to hide his light under a bushel.

At age 80 Birkmayer is a physical marvel. Despite the carcinoma that captured a large part of his tongue, and a history of other ailments, he spends long days seeing patients. Twice a week he plays tennis. Three times a year he takes skiing holidays. He ice-skates. And he enjoys dancing.

Birkmayer was born in Vienna and worked as a physical education instructor before becoming a medical doctor. Between 1936 and 1938 he was a young instructor at the Nerveklinik University in Vienna, and upon the outbreak of World War II he entered the German armed forces, acting as a "head physician."

Birkmayer was injured early in the war and returned to Vienna. In 1943 he once again became a doctor at a military hospital specializing in head injuries, remaining there until 1945. Birkmayer's war record ostracized him from some members of Vienna society in the years following World War II. There are stories in Vienna that Birkmayer felt that the resentment of some members of the medical establishment, particularly those who were Jewish, retarded the later advancement of his career.

Joseph Knoll, who became a colleague with Birkmayer in the clinical testing of deprenyl, prefers not to discuss Birkmayer's personal life. Knoll, who spent most of his teenage years in concentration camps, says of the Birkmayer stories: "It is done. It is finished."[3]

On a warm day in the summer of 1989, in his office in Vienna, Birkmayer was wearing an incongruous turtleneck sweater. He is a small man, but hardly frail for his age. Whatever the controversies that have surrounded him, and however unorthodox his professional methods, it is not hard to imagine Birkmayer being the kind of doctor who inspires responsiveness as well as loyalty from his patients.

---

[3]One U.S. neurologist made inquiries at the Simon Wiesenthal Institute in Washington and was told that Birkmayer was expelled from the SS in Austria prior to World War II when it was learned he was "of mixed blood." According to the same report, Birkmayer was refused membership in the Nazi Party for the same reason after the outbreak of the war.

Birkmayer was entirely candid when he was asked about deprenyl's seeming life-prolonging powers. "I don't know," he said. He also stated that he was surprised when his retrospective analysis revealed that deprenyl appeared to increase life expectancy. "It is not very easy to explain. I can only say that the more levodopa you give to Parkinson's patients, the quicker the degeneration of the dopaminergic nerves. If you can reduce the dosage of levodopa, you can reduce its side effects. Deprenyl does this. But it must be doing something else, as well. What that might be, I don't know."

In North America a group of doctors and scientists was preparing to seek the answers to all the questions about deprenyl. The ultimate test for the drug would be one of the largest clinical trials ever carried out. Orchestrated by the U.S. government's National Institutes of Health, the trial would be conducted at 22 hospitals and universities in the United States and Canada.

It was called the DATATOP study.

10

DESPERATELY SEEKING FDA APPROVAL

DON BUYSKE WAS HEARTENED when he learned of the DATATOP study. He was hopeful that it would furnish proof that deprenyl altered the course of Parkinson's disease. Such a judgment would make deprenyl a major drug. But Buyske did not have time to wait for the results: the DATATOP study would not begin until the summer of 1987 and was to take five years to complete. His imperative was to get deprenyl on the U.S. market as quickly as possible. The only way to do that was to concentrate on the drug's proven use as an adjunct to levodopa therapy.

Buyske's problem was money. In the year ending June 30, 1987, Somerset Pharmaceuticals spent well over one million dollars to sponsor the necessary studies aimed at proving deprenyl's safety and efficacy, but the FDA was still far from satisfied, and

Somerset was running out of funds.

The principal shareholders in Somerset were Wall Street venture capital companies whose objective was a return on their investment. They had not seen any returns yet, and they were certainly not eager to put up any more money.

Throughout the summer of 1987 Buyske negotiated with the FDA. In August he told the FDA that deprenyl had reached "crisis status" and that he might have to give up his efforts to win approval for the drug.

Buyske was not without ammunition. He had a collection of testimonials to deprenyl from the families of patients who had taken the drug under the FDA's investigational exemption. The letter from Corinne Baggett was typical. Mrs. Baggett, who lives near Chicago, had written to her doctor, Claude Fortin, about the effects of deprenyl on her husband:

> I just wanted to tell you that I can't believe how well Bob is doing. You would not believe the personality changes in him. He seems to have such a change in his attitude; he just seems his old self. He laughs, makes jokes, teases, and talks. He just seems like the man I married. It is just *wonderful*!
>
> Thank you for reading this. I just wanted to let you know that I can really see a lot of difference in Bob and so can our sons . . .

Buyske could cite many other cases. Roy Josten, a lawyer in Racine had been diagnosed as parkinsonian at the relative early age of 45. Josten had told a newspaper interviewer about the symptoms of the disease:

You get depressed seeing yourself doing less and less all the time and being more and more tired. You find your world closing in around you. I could see myself going downhill and I worried that it would just be a matter of time before I'd have to give up my law practice.

And then came deprenyl:

I really feel I've gotten better. The tremors in my hands have declined. Instead of sleeping in the afternoons I have energy not only during the day but also at night.[1]

Buyske also had allies in Washington. Morris Udall, who had tried twice to win the Democratic nomination for President of the United States, found he had Parkinson's disease in 1979. Udall was 63 and in his fourteenth term as a congressman when he began taking deprenyl. "I think I'm better off than I was two years ago," he said afterward. "That medicine [deprenyl] makes my days a lot easier."[2]

Perhaps most helpful to Buyske's cause was his network of friends in the medical and scientific fraternities. One was Richard Thompson, a neurologist from Phoenix, Arizona, who himself had Parkinson's. Thompson had read about deprenyl in 1985 and decided to begin his own investigational study on the long-term effects of the drug. Another friend was Dr.

---

[1]Jerry Resler, "Attorney, 49, Is Battling Parkinson's," *Milwaukee Sentinel*, April 26, 1989.

---

[2]"Udall Battles Parkinson's with Humor," *Chandler Arizona Tribune*, June 6, 1987. Further, several members of Congress, at the request of their constituents, had asked the FDA why the approval of deprenyl was taking so long.

Edith Corregano of Brooklyn, who had begun her own investigational trial with deprenyl and found that the drug "had generally favorable results and no adverse side effects of any consequence."

The application to approve the drug had its complications. It still carried the undeserved smirch of the cheese effect that was associated with MAO inhibitors. Deprenyl's pharmacokinetics — the way it worked in the body — were not clear. Amphetamine was locked in the chemical structure of deprenyl, and the FDA wanted to be satisfied that deprenyl did not have addictive properties.

Buyske's application was further complicated by suggestions made by others that deprenyl was a panacea, an all-healing elixir, a concept the FDA will not tolerate. That notion arose from the drug's multiple effects, including its feel-better psychostimulant nature. It had been fed by Walter Birkmayer's longevity study, showing that Parkinson's patients treated with deprenyl could expect to have as much as two years tacked onto their lives. And Joseph Knoll's musings about the brain's dopaminergic system being "the engine of life" further supported the notion.

And then, there was its effects on Alzheimer's disease.

In truth, deprenyl had unusual and sometimes mysterious properties. There seemed to be little rational explanation, for example, why deprenyl should help to relieve the symptoms of Alzheimer's disease. The pathological damage associated with the symptoms of Alzheimer's was removed from the substantia nigra, the region of the brain affected in Parkinson's victims.

Alzheimer's and Parkinson's were both neurodegenerative diseases, but that seemed to be as far as it went. Yet experienced and reputable doctors had used deprenyl to treat Alzheimer's victims, and the drug had wrought positive effects.

The most widely quoted study of the effects of deprenyl on Alzheimer's had been conducted in 1986 by a group of scientists led by Pierre Tariot of the National Institutes of Health. Tariot administered deprenyl to 17 Alzheimer's patients whose ages ranged from 42 to 72. Within 21 days many of the patients showed reduced signs of anxiety/depression and agitation, and there was a trend toward decreases in anergia (lack of energy) and hostility. Approximately half the patients' conditions were judged to be improved clinically, with evidence of increased activity and social interaction along with reduced tension and retardation. "This overall behavioral improvement was associated with cognitive changes. The patients showed improved performance on the most complex episodic memory and learning task that also required sustained attention during treatment with deprenyl."

A member of the research team later described the transformation that occurred in one of the patients. Hilda Gallagher was 65 years old and had suffered from Alzheimer's for four and a half years. Mrs. Gallagher had not communicated with her family since 1984, but had sat in a chair in her daughter's home staring into space. After treatment with deprenyl, she began to show interest in the activities of the hospital ward and attempted to communicate with her family. Back at home she was manageable once again.

Also in 1986, researchers at the National Institute of Nervous and Mental Disease in Budapest had conducted a small pilot study of the effects of deprenyl on seven female Alzheimer's patients. The results were not broken down according to each patient's response, but overall, improvement "was pronounced as regards self-care, short-term memory, mental alertness, and cooperativeness."

Both 1986 studies began from the premise that some postmortem Alzheimer's brains had shown high levels of the MAO B enzyme. The U.S. group had remarked upon the suggestion of Joseph Knoll that overactivity of MAO B might account for some of the symptoms of senescence and that deprenyl had been shown to suppress the chemical reactivity of MAO B.

But it was not clear why deprenyl reduced tension and anxiety in Alzheimer's patients. There were many questions to be answered. Did deprenyl, by perking up the brain's dopaminergic system, relieve stress and pressure on other systems of the brain? Conversely, when one of the brain's systems weaken, do other systems rally to its defense? Was the brain, like the whole body, regulated by a homeostasis that compensates for any functional imbalance?

These speculations might be intriguing, but they did nothing to support Buyske's urgent need to keep Somerset and deprenyl alive. His application to the FDA was for approval of deprenyl as an adjunctive drug in the middle and late stages of Parkinson's disease. Period. Suggestions that the drug might have other applications, other effects, were a distraction. The FDA did not like unsupported claims on behalf of any drug, and they were especially particular when a drug was in the middle of the approval process.

Financial relief came to Don Buyske from an unexpected source. In August 1987 he found Morton Shulman, a Canadian doctor, on his doorstep.

Shulman was unknown to Buyske, but in Canada he was a household name. As chief coroner for the metropolitan area of Toronto, he had interpreted his mandate in the broadest possible way. He not only exposed sloppy procedures in the operating room, but he caused a local expressway to be redesigned and fought the U.S. Air Force for jurisdiction over the wreckage of a downed jet. As an opposition politician, he had been a constant irritant to the governing party of the Province of Ontario. He snapped photographs of cabinet ministers who slept while the legislature was in session, and one day he emptied the government chamber when he walked in with a semiautomatic rifle to demonstrate that firearms were too easily accessible. As a stock market speculator and investor, he had been blacklisted by the investment bankers of Toronto's Bay Street for invading their turf.

Shulman nettled some and endeared himself to others by making it all sound so easy. He made a million dollars by writing a bestselling book about investing called *Anyone Can Make a Million*. He was the model for a popular television series about a doctor who tilted at establishment values. His turreted home was a playground for hedonists.

In the summer of 1981 Shulman was running a medical practice, hosting a weekly confrontation television show, and writing a newspaper column that combined advocacy and muckraking. He was successful, happy and, he thought, healthy.

One day, sitting at his desk, he noticed a slight, persistent tremor in his left leg. He found he could stop it by concentrating on it, but as his attention drifted away the tremor would return. He did not give it much thought until a few weeks later when he began to develop a slight shuffle in his walk. Shulman dug out the medical books and decided he was either developing the early symptoms of Parkinson's disease or had an "essential" tremor — a shakiness that can affect even healthy men and women. In an attempt to soothe the tremor, he began taking a well-known tranquilizing drug. When it had no effect, he realized he might have Parkinson's disease.

For the next few months Shulman was a physician who treated himself. He tried two or three drugs sometimes used in the early stages of the disease. They provided temporary relief, but the symptoms worsened. By September of the same year, 1981, he gave in and visited his own family doctor, who confirmed he had Parkinson's.

His doctor prescribed levodopa, followed a few weeks later by Parlodel, the trade name for bromocriptine, one of the drugs that mimics dopamine in the brain. At first the bromocriptine produced horrible side effects, including nausea, diarrhea, and fainting, but after a while these unpleasant reactions subsided. Shulman's friends noticed he was slow and tentative and that he lacked the zest he had always had. He knew they talked about him among themselves, but they were gracious enough to say nothing to him.

For more than five years he carried on with his life, although at a slower pace. And then, in the spring of 1987, it happened. He began to shake, he was rigid while seated, and frequently his body failed to respond to his commands. He needed assistance to get out of bed and had to use a cane to get around the house. His wife had bars installed on the sides of the bed and next to the bathtub so that he could pull himself out. His handwriting, never good, became tiny and spidery. He became self-conscious going to dinner with friends because he had developed the unpleasant habit of drooling.

In desperation Shulman turned to Dr. Anthony Lang, head of the movement disorders clinic at Toronto Western Hospital. He told Lang he could not go on living unless the doctor could do something to help. He contemplated suicide.

Lang told Shulman about a drug that had been used in Europe for some years. He said there were very positive reports about the drug's effects in Parkinson's disease and that it just might work. It was called deprenyl. Shulman called a friend who was on a wine tour of Europe and asked him to bring back some of the drug. Three days later the friend returned to Toronto with 100 tablets.

Deprenyl's recommended dosage is one pill taken with breakfast and a second pill before dinner. Shulman took his first pill the morning after his friend returned from Europe. It was like a miracle. By noon his tremor had gone. The placebo effect? No. His other symptoms subsided, and he felt a rush of energy. His secretary remarked, "You're working me too hard. I liked you better the other way." His wife made some jokes, too, because of his increased libido. This was a welcome and unexpected side effect.

Shulman wrote a letter to Canada's minister of health and welfare and asked, "Why is deprenyl not allowed to be sold in this country?" The reply was: "We would be delighted to consider an application to qualify deprenyl for sale in Canada. To this date no one has asked."

Here was an opportunity to help other people, as well as make money. Shulman's secretary telephoned the manufacturer of the drug, Chinoin Chemical and

Pharmaceutical Works in Budapest, and asked who held the rights to the drug. They did, they replied, but they had assigned the western hemisphere rights to a company in the United States called Somerset Pharmaceuticals.

The American Pharmaceutical Association was unable to give Shulman any clues about Somerset's existence. It was weeks before he was able to locate the company in the small New Jersey town of Denville. When he did, he was not surprised to learn that it was a private company whose shares were not available to the public. "That doesn't matter," he said. "I still want to invest in your company."

That was how Shulman met Don Buyske. The timing could not have been better. It was early August 1987. Somerset, in the person of Buyske, needed money to survive, and Shulman decided to raise the money by forming a new company and selling shares to the public in Canada. He knew all about those things — investing had been his hobby since he began practicing medicine. Fortunately, in the summer of 1987, the stock market was at a record high and very responsive to shares of new companies. What Shulman could not foresee was that on October 19, 1987, the stock market would have its biggest decline in history.

On August 15, 1987, Shulman flew to Newark, accompanied by his accountant and a stockbroker. At the Newark airport, just outside New York City, they were met by a limousine and driven the 40 miles to Denville. In a small suite of offices located in an industrial park, Shulman had his initial encounter with the imposing presence of Dr. Donald A. Buyske.

Buyske needed money, but the situation was not dire. He had an offer on the table from DeGussa, the pharmaceutical company that owned the right to de-prenyl in West Germany. DeGussa was prepared to pay one million dollars for 15 percent of Somerset. Shulman countered by offering $1.25 million (U.S.), but the $250,000 premium did not seem to Buyske to offset the reputation and resources that would come with an alliance with a giant pharmaceutical company. Shulman bumped his offer to $1.4 million and won. Now he had to find the money.

In Toronto Shulman canvassed family, friends, and acquaintances, soliciting amounts of between $25,000 and $200,000. Within 10 days he amassed $1.5 million, enough to pay Somerset and cover expenses.

Although Buyske had spent some years in Montreal early in his career, it did not occur to him that the Canadian rights to deprenyl might have some separate value.

Shulman would show him how it was done. A new company was incorporated, Deprenyl Research Limited, to acquire the Canadian rights from Somerset. Deprenyl Research would (a) issue 2,600,000 shares to the public, (b) pay 1,400,000 shares to Shulman's group of private investors for their newly acquired 15 percent of Somerset, and (c) pay one million (U.S.) plus another 600,000 shares to Somerset in return for the Canadian rights.

Wood Gundy, Inc., the Canadian investment banking house that handled the sale of the 2,600,000 shares to the public, settled on a price of three dollars per share. Out of the total proceeds of $7,800,000 (Cdn.), Deprenyl Research would remit to Somerset the $1,000,000 (U.S.) cash that was part payment for the Canadian rights to the drug.

At the arbitrary share price of three dollars, it didn't take a lot of arithmetic to figure out that Shulmans's private group of investors would receive the equivalent of $4,200,000 (Cdn.) in return for the 15 percent interest in Somerset that had cost them only $1,400,000 (U.S.). But the public was hungry for the stock — Wood Gundy had to limit allotments to its customers — and it seemed like a good deal all around.

When the stock market crashed on October 19, 1987, Wood Gundy got cold feet The public was departing the market in droves, and investors had become especially allergic to new, speculative stock issues. Wood Gundy hastily reported that the pent-up demand for shares of Deprenyl Research had evaporated.

"Don't abandon the issue," Shulman ordered. "I'll sell it myself." And he did. Over the next few months he called everyone he knew, and a lot of people he didn't know, and begged them to buy shares.

On February 9, 1988, shares of Deprenyl Research began trading on the public market. The first shares changed hands not at the issue price of three dollars but at five. A month later the price rose to nine and a half dollars.[3]

Buyske cajoled the FDA and asked his scientist friends to speak up on behalf of deprenyl. A group of doctors at the National Institutes of Health told Buyske they were in favor of the drug, "but no official position of NIH will be expressed."

In a last-ditch telephone conversation with the FDA's director of neuropharmacological drug products, Buyske asked what he had to do to circumvent

---

[3]Shares of Deprenyl Research Limited were eventually listed on the Toronto Stock Exchange. In December 1989 they sold for as high as $18.50.

the FDA requirement for a one-year toxicology study in two animal species. He was told: "Your application has two separate studies of only six months in two species — rats and dogs. Our regulations on a normal drug require a one-year toxicology study. The FDA has never made an exception to this requirement and we must be careful in setting a precedent. The FDA is aware that in European countries six-month toxicology studies are acceptable, but we simply require more." The FDA director was sympathetic: "I am not concerned about the safety of deprenyl [but] it is still a problem for the FDA to modify long-established standards."[4]

Much later the FDA did begin to change some of its standards in response to intense lobbying by AIDS victims who were anxious to be given access to drugs whose toxicity had not been fully tested. The controversy over granting fast approval for AIDS drugs gave Don Buyske an opening he could not resist. "How would you like it," he asked Dr. Frank Young, an FDA commissioner, "if 10 busloads of old ladies with tennis shoes and Parkinson's disease parked on your front doorstep?"

By 1988 deprenyl had a long history of safe administration in the treatment of Parkinson's disease. In Europe the drug had been used for 150 thousand patient-years. Most people who had taken deprenyl felt better as a result, and there had been no serious adverse side effects. In the United States, while deprenyl

---

[4]In 1970 Sinemet, a levodopa preparation, was approved 30 days after making application to the FDA due to its successful use in England and Europe. Deprenyl, with similar success in England and Europe, required 6 years and tests costing tens of millions of dollars. A striking example of Lord Acton's comment regarding absolute power.

was still an experimental drug, more and more doctors were using it under investigational exemptions from the FDA.

Deprenyl was a proven therapeutic agent. When used *with* levodopa, deprenyl not only lessened symptoms but reduced the side effects associated with continued use of levodopa. It prolonged the efficacy of levodopa and smoothed out the erratic responses to levodopa treatment.

The first U.S. doctor to prescribe deprenyl had been Melvin Yahr, chairman of the department of neurology at New York's Mount Sinai School of Medicine. Yahr had first applied to the FDA for an investigational exemption in 1979, and in the succeeding few years his interest in deprenyl helped to keep alive the changes that the drug would someday be approved for general use in the United States.

Yahr casts a long shadow and has sometimes been called the dean of U.S. neurologists. Born in 1917 in New York City, he embarked on a career that influenced the direction of research in many of the major disorders of the central nervous system. In the past 30 years he has written on every aspect of Parkinson's disease — pathology, its symptoms, and its treatments.

"In the 1950s," Yahr says, "you couldn't get 10 doctors to attend a meeting on Parkinson's disease. There just wasn't much new to talk about." Research into the cause and treatment of PD was at a dead end. That all changed with the discoveries that led to the development of levodopa. After levodopa there was a lot of jockeying for recognition in the scientific community, "a lot of one-upmanship," as Yahr puts it, "and a lot of chins out of joint."

Yahr knew and was respected by all of the major

players in the levodopa story. In fact, he knew every-
one in the forefront of research into Parkinson's
disease. He had first met Joseph Knoll in 1978 at the
CINP Congress Collegium Internationale Neuro-
Psychopharmacologicum in Vienna. Yahr and Walter
Birkmayer were co-chairmen of this scientific gather-
ing, the first at which deprenyl was the major topic.
Unfortunately the congress was attended mostly by
European scientists and attracted little attention in the
United States. Yahr again encountered Knoll at a
meeting of the Hungarian Pharmacological Society in
Budapest in 1979. That same year he began prescribing
deprenyl to his patients in the United States.

Throughout the early 1980s, Don Buyske relied on
the work of Melvin Yahr to keep deprenyl in front of
the scientific community. It is as a clinician that Yahr is
best known — the type of doctor skilled at observing
changes brought about by drugs and other therapies.
Buyske was supported by Yahr's clinical investigations into the effects of the drug.

It is impossible to summarize accurately all of Yahr's
investigations into deprenyl, but the results of his
studies are best expressed in the publication of one of
his papers in 1983:

Deprenyl's major usefulness . . . has been
demonstrated in patients under treatment
with levodopa, which has become complicated by fluctuating responses — particularly
those of the end-start-dose variety. In such
patients it is possible to achieve an increase in
'on' time and a decrease in the severity of
parkinsonism. In most patients such a re-

sponse can be maintained for a period of two years or longer."[5]

Starting in 1983, Buyske began to assemble the detailed results of clinical studies around the world that used deprenyl as an adjuvant to levodopa treatment. These studies, he believed, would help to persuade the FDA of both the safety and efficacy of deprenyl.

In Milan, Italy, a group of doctors at the Institution Neurologica reported after a 10-week study that deprenyl had resulted in a "significant improvement" in patients in the middle stage of Parkinson's disease, although there were "no significant modification of symptoms" in the latter stage of the disease. In Helsinki, Finland, doctors at the University of Turku said that deprenyl "appears to be a useful adjuvant to Levodopa in patients with daily fluctuations in disability." In Oslo, Norway, doctors at the Ulleval Hospital came to the conclusion that "with deprenyl, the levodopa dosage can be reduced considerably without prejudicing the therapeutic outcome."

Buyske had hoped the passage of the Orphan Drug Act would expedite approval of deprenyl. The new law had encouraged him to acquire the rights to deprenyl in the first place. But if he thought the act would lead to speedy approval of deprenyl, he was sadly disappointed.

The intent of the U.S. Congress in passing the Orphan Drug Act in 1983 had been to reduce the enormous amount of data normally required by the

---

[5]"Treatment of Parkinson's Disease in Early and Late Phases: Use of Pharmacological Agents with Special Reference to Deprenyl (Selegiline)," *Acta Neurol. Scand.* (Denmark, 1983).

FDA for the approval of certain drugs. The FDA had testified before Congress that in the case of orphan drugs, the agency would apply common sense and understanding in the criteria used to measure safety and efficacy. In the case of deprenyl, the FDA required full compliance, with the usual demands for large volumes of detailed studies in humans as well as in animals. This decision by the FDA added several million dollars to Somerset's cost of winning approval and delayed deprenyl's availability on the U.S. market by an additional three years.

It was not that Buyske and Somerset Pharmaceuticals had failed to put pressure on the government. Through the many investigational exemptions granted to individual doctors, the FDA was already well aware that there was a swell of demand — from doctors and patients alike — for approval of deprenyl.

Physician INDs — Claimed Investigational Exemptions — had by now been used in the case of deprenyl by many doctors in the United States. The evidence assembled so far, as to the safety and effectiveness of the drug, was sufficient to prompt Somerset to apply for a "treatment" IND, the second, optional phase in the investigation of new drugs. It allows a commercial sponsor, such as Somerset, to recruit private physicians and to supply the drug in question for use by their patients.

By setting in motion a treatment IND, Buyske found himself unintentionally with a group of 1,000 patients, which became a powerful lobby for deprenyl. But the FDA was adamant that it would grant "no special priority" for deprenyl.

Yes, there were many European studies whose results testified to the safety and efficacy of deprenyl.

And, yes, there were U.S. studies that had achieved the same results. But none of the U.S. studies were controlled. None were double-blind. In none of the existing studies was the response of deprenyl-treated patients properly compared with patients using another therapy.

The FDA insisted on the kind of clinical evidence that could only come from a controlled study. Furthermore, to be credible, such a study would have to be double-blind — neither the patients nor the doctors would know whether each patient was taking deprenyl or the "control" therapy.

Buyske proposed that Somerset would sponsor the study, and that it would be designed to answer all of the FDA's outstanding concerns. Finally it was agreed that the study would consist of a two-week "baseline" period to record the disability of patients prior to deprenyl treatment, and then a six-period during which neurologists would prescribe deprenyl and monitor effects.

Buyske needed three neurologists with impeccable credentials to conduct the study. He found Roger Duvoisin, Abraham Lieberman, and Manfred Muenter. The name of Duvoisin, a professor at the Robert Wood Johnson Medical School in New Jersey, had long graced the literature of Parkinson's disease. Lieberman, a professor of neurology and an attending physician at a number of New York City hospitals, had written and lectured extensively on Parkinson's disease. Muenter was a member of the department of neurology at the Mayo Clinic in Rochester, Minnesota.

With Duvoisin, Buyske traveled to Washington and met with Paul Leber, director of neuropharmacological drug products, along with a dozen or so members of

Leber's staff. Here were assembled the FDA's experts in clinical design, chemistry, toxicology, and all the other disciplines that would help to decide deprenyl's bona fides. The result was a study entitled "Deprenyl in the Treatment of Symptom Fluctuations in Advanced Parkinson's Disease."[6]

Its summary, in part, reads as follows:

> Deprenyl, a selective inhibitor of monoamine oxidase, type B, which is free of the "tyramine effect" (the "cheese effect") may ameliorate symptom fluctuations in advanced Parkinson's disease (PD): We randomized 96 patients with marked symptom fluctuations at three centers to receive either deprenyl . . . or placebo in parallel fashion in addition to previously optimized levodopa/carbidopa (Sinemet) regimen.

> Disability was recorded hourly at home by patients three days weekly during the two-week baseline and the six-week treatment period.

> Disability during the "on" state was assessed each week by examination. Mean hourly self-assessment of gait improved in 28 of 50 patients (56%) receiving deprenyl and in 14 of 46 patients (30.4%) taking placebo. Mean hourly overall symptom control improved in 29 (58%) taking deprenyl and in 12 (26.1%) taking placebo.

---

[6]Published in *Clinical Neuropharmacology*, Vol. II, No. 1, 45-55 (New York: Raven Press, 1988).

> Mean daily Sinemet dosage decreases were 17% in the deprenyl group and 7% in the placebo group.
>
> Adverse effects included nausea, light-headedness, dyskinesias, and hallucinations, all of which abated after the Sinemet dose was reduced.
>
> We conclude that deprenyl is of moderate benefit in a majority of patients with symptom fluctuations complicating PD and is generally well tolerated.

The logjam with the FDA had been broken. Deprenyl had passed the FDA's test. A test that measured what everyone in England and Europe had known for many years — deprenyl slows the progress of Parkinson's disease, improves the patients motor abilities and their sense of well being.

Meanwhile, the role of the dopaminergic system — and the part deprenyl played in supporting the health of this system — was the subject of much serious speculation in the case of Alzheimer's disease. By 1989 the prevalence of the disease was even more widespread than previously suspected. A study conducted by the Harvard Medical School one of the largest and most detailed ever attempted on the subject, found that 10 percent of people in the United States over age 65 had memory impairment or other mental problems for which the most likely cause was deemed to be Alzheimer's.

The Harvard study found that a startling 47 percent of those older than 85 probably had the disease. That finding doubled previous estimates and, if applied to older people throughout the United States, would raise the estimated number of Alzheimer's cases to four million people from what was thought to be 2.5 million people. By 1989 deprenyl had been "implicated" as a possible treatment for Alzheimer's.

There were reasons to believe that deprenyl had no effect on the pathological disturbances associated with Alzheimer's — those senile plaques and fibrillary tangles that seemed not to be linked to the dopaminergic system. On the other hand, those same disturbances were present in the brains of many elderly people, and much more likely to be present, and in greater numbers, in the brains of Parkinson's victims.

And then there was deprenyl's power to reduce tension and anxiety in some Alzheimer's patients.

In 1988 doctors at the University of California School of Medicine put to the test previous findings that deprenyl had the effects in Alzheimer's patients of decreasing anxiety, tension, depression and excitement, improved reaction time, continuous performance, and recall.

They chose as clinical subjects 15 males and females, 60 years or older. All but one completed four weeks of deprenyl treatment without side effects. Among the patient group there were "significant decreases in sadness, irritability, and agitation." As well, there was a modest improvement in recall of recent events by most of the patients.

In Alzheimer's the ideal therapy would be one that prevented or halted progression of the disease. In the absence of such a therapy, which would subvert the cognitive/memory deficits that are hallmarks of the disease, doctors are beginning to concentrate on be-

181

havioral, noncognitive aspects. The nearer term objective is to relieve the psychosis, depression, and agitation that almost invariably accompany the onset of Alzheimer's.

Although the cognitive/memory deficits devastate victims of Alzheimer's and their families, it is the associated behavioral problems that ultimately force the care givers to seek institutional care in spite of the attendant enormous economic costs. Even if deprenyl were to have no bearing on the course of Alzheimer's disease, or even its cognitive/memory symptoms, deprenyl would be of great value if it helped to subdue the behavioral manifestations of Alzheimer's.

All of the major studies conducted to date suggested that deprenyl was that kind of drug — it improved the quality of life, it made Alzheimer's patients more manageable, and it increased the chances for home versus institutional care. None of this had anything to do with Buyske's pending application before the FDA to have deprenyl approved as an adjunctive drug in the middle and late stages of Parkinson's disease; it was just another dimension of this miracle drug.

———————————*———————————

Sixty-seven people were in attendance at the meeting on March 31, 1989, in the auditorium of the Toronto Stock Exchange. Morty Shulman acted as greeter. Wearing a light gray suit, he was in his element as he pronounced, in a staccato voice, "This is the first annual meeting of Deprenyl Research Limited . . ."

A slide presentation then showed the potential uses of deprenyl:

Parkinsonism: adjunctive agent
Parkinsonism: to slow progress of the disease
Alzheimer's: behavioral symptoms
Depression —

Shulman was in his element. And why not? He himself had been given a reprieve by deprenyl, and many other people, not all of them his patients, had expressed their gratitude to him for transforming their lives. He deserved reward.

Typical of the testimonials that arrived at his home or office was a letter from Martin Siegerman, a senior officer of the Royal Bank of Canada:

> . . . I again want to tell you what absolutely magical effects Eldepryl has had on me. After seven or eight years of inexorable deterioration, my Parkinson's symptoms were reaching a level of serious incapacitation, with all the classic problems becoming more severe. Eldepryl has reduced or eliminated the various symptoms and has, I feel, released me from a cage. I want to thank you for bringing this wonderful medication to the community at large and to me personally. It has brought me dramatic relief and I am very grateful.

In the United States Somerset Pharmaceuticals attracted takeover offers from major pharmaceutical companies. Don Buyske's partners, the venture capitalists from Wall Street, did not wait to seize their opportunity to make a profit on their investment. They did not realize that, had they had a little more patience, they could have had much more.

At three o'clock one morning Morty Shulman awoke with a start. He turned to his wife Gloria and said, "I've got the idea of a lifetime!" His idea was to add deprenyl to pet food. Deprenyl had added years to his own life. In Vienna Walter Birkmayer had reported that deprenyl extended the life span of victims of Parkinson's disease. In Budapest Joseph Knoll said that deprenyl not only increased the life span of aged rats but also reawakened their interest in sex.

People loved pets. The market for pet food with deprenyl added would be enormous — the drug could be added to the diets of dogs and cats and other household animals. Who would not take a chance that just a little bit of deprenyl would extend the life of beloved Fido? The royalties would come pouring in and they could prove deprenyl's life extension properties within a relatively short time. Shulman formed a new company, a subsidiary of Deprenyl Research Limited called DEPL Animal Food Supplement, and prepared to sell shares to the public.[7]

The FDA was not amused. The Directors of Somerset Pharmaceuticals, most especially the outside directors, feared the pet food project would delay final FDA approval for the use of deprenyl in humans. Furthermore, Somerset had an offer on the table from Sandoz Pharmaceutical Corporation for more than $30 million. That offer might now be in jeopardy as a result of the idea to feed deprenyl to household pets.

Shulman, irrepressible as ever, made what was seen as another faux pas. He leaked information of the Sandoz takeover bid and said that it was not enough.

---

[7] In October 1992, a patent was granted to Animal Health Inc., of Overland Kansas for the use of deprenyl in treating animals.

He would be prepared to pay more for Somerset Pharmaceuticals. "This drug [deprenyl] shows the promise of doing incredible things. Why give it away for a few million?" He was convinced that Somerset would be worth much more after there were further investigations into deprenyl's life-prolonging powers. "The longevity thing," he pronounced, "is mind-boggling."

The last straw, as far as some of his partners in Somerset Pharmaceutical were concerned, was when Shulman jumped the gun on the announcement of pending FDA approval for deprenyl. On April 11, 1989, he sent out a press release announcing that the FDA was about to announce an approvability notice for deprenyl. (This was the penultimate step to final approval: all that remained to be negotiated was the wording of the package insert, or labeling, which must include all of the material information about a drug — positive and negative.) The FDA liked to make its own announcements. What was Shulman's hurry?

Morty Shulman had one eye on the stock market. Of that there was no doubt. Shares of Deprenyl Research Limited, of which he and his family owned the majority of shares, rose to more than $15 in the summer of 1989. He had a valid argument for announcing the approvability letter — it was a material event that could (and did) affect the share price of Deprenyl Research Limited. On the other hand, it was not his business to make the announcement. "I'll keep my mouth shut from now on," he later told a newspaper reporter. The FDA announced its approval of deprenyl in June, 1989. The first three paragraphs of a press release issued by the Department of Health and Human Services were as follows:

The FDA today announced approval of a drug called selegiline [the chemical name for deprenyl] to help treat severe Parkinson's disease, a degenerative disorder of the central nervous system with symptoms that include slowness of movement, muscular rigidity, and an instability that frequently leads to falls.

Selegiline would be added to the standard therapy using the drug levodopa, which often decreases in effectiveness even with increased doses.

Currently, as levodopa's effectiveness fades, either Parkinson's debilitating symptoms return or higher doses are required to suppress them, with increasingly severe side effects. But selegiline, which differs in its mode of action, has proved useful in controlled clinical studies in maintaining function despite use of lower doses of levodopa, without increased side effects . . .

"Different mode of action," said the press release. What was this different mechanism?

Much of the confusion about deprenyl arose from the differences in its effects on two fairly distinct groups of Parkinson's patients. Parkinson's disease has three stages. The early stage lasts from the time the disease is first diagnosed until the symptoms become disabling. At this point, levodopa is called into play — to substitute for the role of the missing dopamine in the brain and to relieve the accompanying symptoms.

The middle stage is that period, typically between three and six years, during which the patient responds favorably to levodopa therapy. The late stage of Parkinson's disease is the period after which levodopa loses most of its positive effects. Despite increasing doses, the effects of levodopa can wear off suddenly, or the patient suffers on-off effects. It is during the late stage of the disease that the side effects of levodopa frequently become uncomfortable, and sometimes intolerable.

In the early stage of the disease, before levodopa becomes necessary to calm symptoms, patients are said to be "untreated."[8] It is after levodopa treatment begins — in the middle and late stages of Parkinson's disease — that deprenyl may be used to sustain and enhance the effects of levodopa and to mitigate levodopa's side effects.

The therapeutic value of deprenyl had been proven to the FDA in this category of patients — the levodopa group of patients — when deprenyl was used as an *adjuvant* drug.

To prove to the FDA deprenyl's ability to protect the dopaminergic system and thereby protect people from disabling diseases as Parkinson's, was not even attempted. It would have been utterly futile. However, this is exactly what was proven by the DATATOP study.

---

[8]At the first diagnosis of Parkinson's disease, antidepressants may be prescribed and palliative remedies may be applied. Nonetheless, a Parkinson's patient is said to be "untreated" until the time of levodopa therapy.

11

THE DATATOP STUDY

✴ AT THE APRIL 1985 MEETING of the American Academy of Neurology in Dallas, Texas, Ira Shoulson and Stanley Fahn convened an informal meeting to talk about the prospect for preventative therapies for Parkinson's disease. Until then, all treatments for PD were symptomatic: the development of levodopa and other drugs that mimicked the action of dopamine had represented a major breakthrough in the treatment of PD patients. In most patients these therapies had resulted in a temporary amelioration of symptoms and disability, and even an increase in life span. But levodopa and other "dopaminergic" drugs — replacement therapies that made up for the deficiency of dopamine in the brain — gave only transient relief. Eventually parkinsonian features worsened as the brain cells in the substantia nigra continued to wear out and die. Shoulson and Fahn agreed that it was time to start looking at measures that might protect against the degeneration of these cells and thereby halt or at least forestall the progress of the disease.

It was time to shift the strategy from symptomatic therapy to preventative therapy. The target would be the underlying pathological cause of the disease, not just its symptoms.

Shoulson was from the University of Rochester, Fahn from Columbia University in New York City. Both were well known neurologists in the community of Parkinson's disease specialists. With some of their colleagues in a Dallas hotel room, the doctors took their bearings.

If the cause of Parkinson's disease were known, the prevention or cure would be readily at hand. But so far the cause was a mystery. The disease was almost certainly not the result of a virus or other infection. Genetic predisposition had been disproven. What else could cause a disease that was so common?

Poison was left as the most likely culprit, a poison or poisons either manufactured within the body or introduced from the environment. While there was no clue what that poison might be, it might be possible to determine the mechanism by which it damaged the brain. If the mechanism were known, then it might be possible to use drugs to block it.

Recent animal and human studies had suggested that, whatever the putative poison, the reason cells broke down was because of some kind of oxidative action in the brain. Oxygen is essential for animal life, but oxidative processes within nerve cells and oxidative events caused by certain environmental substances might lead to dopamine cell loss and the eventual signs of PD. Shoulson and Fahn concluded that this was the best basis for a hypothesis, and they reviewed the evidence.

Andre Barbeau, the Montreal neurologist, had recently published data linking high prevalence of Parkinson's disease in regions of Quebec with high exposure to agricultural pesticides. Barbeau's study was considered the most compelling evidence that PD was caused by an environmental toxin. But even if this were the case, why would some people succumb to the toxin and others not? Perhaps it was because some people could not withstand the same oxidative stress tolerated by others. Or maybe the problem lay in the brain's mechanisms.

There was much support for this theory. First of all, it had been shown that the inactivation of dopamine by a process of oxidation resulted in the formation of hydrogen peroxide and other free radicals. Such free radicals — molecules without a home — were capable of cellular damage. It could be argued that whatever the toxic substance that triggered the production of free radicals, it was the oxidative mechanisms that predisposed some people to the loss of dopamine cells.

Second, it was known that a pigmented chemical called lipofuscin tended to show up in greater proportions in the urine of older people. Formation of lipofuscin was thought to result from the activity of free radicals. Lipofuscin, structurally and chemically, was very similar to another substance called neuromelanin, which was responsible for the black hue of cells in a healthy substantia nigra. Some doctors postulated that the accumulation of neuromelanin promoted cellular dysfunction. The theory that free radicals were implicated in the brain damage associated with the symptoms of Parkinson's disease was reinforced by information that came from the examination of postmortem brains of PD sufferers. In the substantia nigra of these brains there was a shortage of the chemical scavengers that attacked free radical molecules. And there was the story of MPTP, the drug that had induced parkinsonism in a group of young heroin addicts in California.

Shoulson and Fahn arrived at the conclusion that, notwithstanding the identity of the poison that might bring about Parkinson's disease, it could be argued that the disease arose out of a heightened or accelerated susceptibility to oxidative processes within the body. It was agreed at the meeting in Dallas that the only way to test these theories effectively was through a major clinical trial involving many patients and conducted at a large number of hospitals in the United States and Canada. Shoulson and Fahn agreed to organize the planning for such an effort. They would be the principal investigators.

The first strategy meeting of what became known as the Parkinson Study Group was held two months later at the University of Rochester. Position papers were developed to deal with the rationale and design for the study. One of the tasks was to develop a unified rating scale so that all of the doctors in the clinical trial would use the same criteria in monitoring the progress of patients. Another issue was: which drug or drugs would be used in the trial?

Back in 1979 Fahn himself had begun to experiment with high-dose chronic vitamin E therapy in the treatment of Parkinson's disease. The active form of vitamin E, called tocopherol, was known to protect cells and their covering membranes from damage due to oxidative processes.

Fahn prescribed vitamin E to a number of PD patients who were in the early stages of the disease and did not yet require levodopa therapy. The results indicated that patients who took the vitamin E supplement were able to last longer than others before their symptoms became bothersome enough to require levodopa therapy. But these results were not conclusive because Fahn's experiments were not controlled. There was no "control" group of patients against whom he could compare the experience of his vitamin E patients.

Although Fahn's results were not scientifically reliable, they were certainly highly suggestive. He had also reassured himself that a chronic high-dose vitamin E regimen was safe. A few patients had complained of temporary indigestion, but adverse effects were almost nonexistent.

The Parkinson Study Group decided that vitamin E, or tocopherol, would be one of the substances they would use to examine the effects of oxidative processes on the death of cells in the substantia nigra.

The second therapy they chose was deprenyl.

Deprenyl seemed to have a more specific antioxidative effect. As an MAO inhibitor, it seemed to discourage the degradation of dopamine, the neurotransmitter whose absence was associated with the presence of Parkinson's disease.

Deprenyl, too, had been proven to be a safe drug. The most persuasive argument in favor of the drug came from a study whose results were published in 1983 under the title "Deprenyl Leads to Prolongation of L-Dopa Efficiency in Parkinson's Disease."[1] The authors of this study, among whom were Joseph Knoll of Budapest and Walter Birkmayer of Vienna, had con-

---

[1] Birkmayer, W., Knoll, J., et al, "Deprenyl Leads to Prolongation of L-Dopa Efficiency in Parkinson's Disease," *Modern Problems of Pharmacological Psychiatry*, Vol. 19, 170-76.

cluded that deprenyl sustained the benefits of levodopa and mitigated its side effects.

If deprenyl allowed PD patients to continue taking
levodopa for a longer period of time, the inescapable
inference was that it helped to conserve the stores of
dopamine in the brain. In other words, deprenyl was
protecting against the oxidative metabolism of dopamine.

Vitamin E (tocopherol), had been chosen as the substance that would be used to test the mechanisms that
led to enhancement of the free radical scavenger system. At the same time, deprenyl was chosen to be the
drug that would allow investigators to examine the
inhibiting effects on the oxidation of dopamine.

Both vitamin E, the free radical antioxidant, and deprenyl, the MAO inhibitor, had already been the
subject of studies that showed they ameliorated disability and slowed the clinical decline of Parkinson's
disease. But all of these studies suffered from a common pitfall of pilot investigations: while offering encouragement, they were both uncontrolled studies.

The Parkinson Study Group wanted to conduct a
study that wold leave no doubts. They wanted a controlled study. To remove any possibility of bias, the
therapeutic effects of the experimental drugs would be
compared to the results of standard therapy. Using this
technique, it would be possible to make an honest, objective evaluation of the outcomes of both types of
therapy.

Since there was no proven therapy to halt the progression of Parkinson's disease, the control drug
would be a placebo, an inactive substance that would
be prepared in an identical form to the active experimental drugs — in this case, deprenyl and tocopherol.

And to guard further against bias, the new trial would be "double-blind" — neither the patients nor the doctors would be aware which drug was being used until the study was concluded.

Members of the Parkinson Study Group reconvened in December 1985 at Columbia University. The question was: how would the doctors measure whether tocopherol and/or deprenyl were having the anticipated effect of slowing down Parkinson's disease?

There had to be a variable. They could not simply peer into the brains of their patients to record the well-being of the dopaminergic cells. Parkinson's is a symptomatic disease: the only way to track its progress is by observing the growing severity of its symptoms. The variable, it was decided, would be "time until levodopa therapy is required."

If a patient taking tocopherol and/or deprenyl could postpone the need for levodopa longer than an untreated patient, then one or the other of those two drugs might be said to be protecting against the cellular loss that was associated with the symptoms of the disease. Hence, the primary response variable — "The time until levodopa is required to treat disability."

The question of sample size was also considered. The results of any human trial are subject to error: the more patients involved, the lower the chance of error. It was agreed that between 700 and 1,000 patients would need to be recruited to remove all but the remotest possibility of error. This decision prompted the need to expand the number of participating institutions to 28 hospitals and universities.

During its meeting at Columbia University, the gathering of doctors and consultants decided to call itself the Parkinson Study Group or PSG for short. Their clinical research study would be the largest ever conducted into the treatment of Parkinson's disease — in fact, one of the largest ever conducted into the treatment of any disease. The name of the study would be Deprenyl and Tocopherol Antioxidative Therapy Of Parkinsonism or DATATOP.

The new study would prove — or disprove — the following hypothesis:

> ... that chronic deprenyl and/or alpha toco-
> pherol (vitamin E) antioxidative therapies
> will slow the progressive degeneration of
> substantia nigra neurons and resulting clin-
> ical decline of Parkinson's disease. Our
> primary aim is to determine whether or not
> chronic deprenyl and/or vitamin E adminis-
> tration to early, otherwise untreated Parkin-
> son's disease patients will prolong the time
> until levodopa therapy is required to treat
> supervening disability.

Two months later at the University of Virginia the growing contingent of members of the PSG unanimously agreed to move ahead with an application to raise the necessary funds. The best estimate was that they needed $10 million. It could come from only one place — the National Institutes of Health.

Ten miles outside Washington, D.C., north on Connecticut Avenue, 40 buildings sprawl across a campus of 300 acres in the neighboring state of Maryland. This is the headquarters of the National Institutes of Health, a medical research organization whose scope surpasses that of any other in the world.

The National Institutes of Health is the all-embracing term for one of the five health agencies of the U.S. Public Health Service, which, in turn, is part of the U.S. Department of Health and Human Services. With an annual budget of more than six billion dollars, its employees search for new ways to help prevent, detect, diagnose, and treat every conceivable disease and disability, from the rarest genetic disorder to the common cold. The NIH has financed the training of one-third of the biomedical researchers in the United States, and it has sponsored the work of two-thirds of those U.S. scientists who have won Nobel prizes for physiology or medicine since 1945. It is the center and pride of America's medical research effort.

DATATOP systematically examined the potential symptomatic and protective effects of deprenyl and tocopherol (vitamin E) in patients who were in the early stage of Parkinson's disease. Eight hundred patients with early signs of Parkinson's disease were enrolled between September 1987 and November 1988.[2] The research subjects were randomly assigned to one of four groups that would receive the following therapies: (a) deprenyl, (b) tocopherol, (c) deprenyl and tocopherol, or (d) placebo. As a double-blind study, neither the investigating doctors nor the patients knew which patients were receiving which therapies.

The co-principal investigators of DATATOP, Ira Shoulson and Stanley Fahn, had discussed the best way of measuring the progress of Parkinson's disease. Direct examination of the brain's dopaminergic cells was not possible. There were some new biological techniques of measuring the decay of cells in the substantia nigra, but these were still unproven.

---

[2] Of this number, 106 were treated at Canadian institutions.

Shoulson and Fahn and their colleagues decided that the best way to measure the progress of the disease was by clinical means — doctors experienced in the treatment of Parkinson's disease would evaluate each patient at three-month intervals and render a judgment as to whether or not the patient had developed sufficient disability to require levodopa treatment. That was the response variable — "the time until levodopa is judged necessary to treat parkinsonian disability." The "baseline" evaluation occurred at the first diagnosis of Parkinson's disease. The "end point" was the time at which the symptoms of the disease became sufficiently disabling to require levodopa treatment. If it turned out that deprenyl (and/or tocopherol) significantly forestalled the need for levodopa, the DATATOP researchers could draw their own inferences about what the drug might be doing to the cells of the substantia nigra.

With so many doctors involved, and given the trickiness of monitoring PD symptoms, it was necessary to give some definition to the term *time until levodopa therapy is required.* The major criteria became threatened or actual erosion of functional capacities related to employability, domestic responsibilities, and gain performance.

Two of the 38 DATATOP investigators were William Langston and his colleague James Tetrud of the California Parkinson's Foundation. Langston and Tetrud had begun their own pilot study of deprenyl in 1986. It was a study similar in design to that of DATATOP, but, of course, it was much smaller, involving 100 patients.

Results of the DATATOP study were not to be released until the summer of 1992, but Langston and Tetrud made the findings of their independent study long before then. In fact, results of the Langston-Tetrud study made a big splash in the media. On August 4, 1989, at the top of page one of the *New York Times*, the headline read: RESEARCHERS FIND NEW DRUG SLOWS PARKINSON'S PACE. The story began as follows:

> A new drug slows the progress of Parkinson's disease, a crippling neurological disorder, researchers reported yesterday.
>
> This is the first time that any drug has been shown to delay the symptoms of any neurological disease. Existing treatments for Parkinson's disease and other neurological conditions have focused on relieving symptoms, neurologists said.
>
> Experts on neurological diseases said they were elated by the findings, and some said they would prescribe the drug for their patients as soon as it becomes available . . .

The *New York Times* story was based on an article that had been published in a recent issue of *Science* magazine. It was entitled "The Effect of Deprenyl on the Natural History of Parkinson's Disease," and its authors were James Tetrud and William Langston.

Tetrud-Langston reported the effects of deprenyl not on the 100 patients originally planned for their pilot study, but on only 54 patients. This was too small a study to be regarded as other than preliminary and in need of confirmation, but the findings were startling.

The authors found that early-stage patients with Parkinson's disease lasted an average of 312 days before levodopa therapy was required. Patients treated with deprenyl did not require levodopa until the lapse of 549 days. "Therefore, early deprenyl therapy delays the requirement for anti-parkinsonian medication, possibly by slowing progression of the disease."

The data also suggested that deprenyl slowed the worsening of the disease by between 40 and 83 percent:

> At least three conclusions can be drawn from this study. First, deprenyl appears to be a remarkably safe drug in patients with early, untreated Parkinson's disease. We failed to observe any serious side effects, and the minor complications that did occur were almost evenly divided between the placebo and deprenyl groups. Second, early deprenyl therapy significantly delays the need for treatment with levodopa. Finally, deprenyl appears to slow the rate of progression of Parkinson's disease as monitored by five different clinical measures. The latter two observations support the hypothesis that deprenyl slows the progression of Parkinson's disease.

The Tetrud-Langston article went on to say: "These issues are not minor, as setting a precedent for one age-related human neurogenerative disease is likely to have consequences for others, such as Alzheimer's disease and amyotrophic lateral sclerosis."

In response to the article in *Science* magazine, the *New York Times* reported that one doctor, Christopher Goetz of Rushmore Presbyterian-St. Luke's Medical Center in Chicago, said, "The concept that you can prevent the natural progression of a neurological disease is revolutionary." Another doctor, Warren Olanow of the University of South Florida, called the results of the Tetrud-Langston study "terrifically exciting." Olanow added, "You can imagine how delighted those of us in the field are to see this result."

In spite of all the euphoria, everyone agreed, including Tetrud and Langston, that more definitive evidence would come from the DATATOP study. Langston and Tetrud had only touched on the possible "mechanisms" by which deprenyl had achieved its effects; DATATOP would deal more fully with that question.

The DATATOP study would continue until 1992, although it would be unfair to deny those patients on placebo the benefits of deprenyl. Therefore, the study was appropriately modified and the interim DATATOP results were published in the *New England Journal of Medicine*, which began:

> Parkinson's disease is a progressively disabling illness that results primarily from the degeneration of dopaminergic neurons in the substantia nigra. The disease symptoms are ameliorated by treatment with levodopa and other dopamine agonists, but the illness progresses and dopaminergic therapies are often attended by adverse effects on motor function and mental state. Most investigators agree that levodopa therapy should be withheld in patients with early Parkinson's disease until its use is warranted by the severity of functional disability. A survey study has indicated that approximately 75 percent of such patients require levodopa therapy

within two years of their initial evaluation
(diagnosis) . . .

The primary objective of our ongoing controlled clinical trial, Deprenyl and Tocopherol
Antioxidative Therapy of Parkinsonism (DA-
TATOP), is to determine whether in patients
with early, untreated Parkinson's disease
long-term therapy with deprenyl or tocopherol extends the interval before the severity
of disability requires the initiation of levodopa therapy.

The interim results lead to the following conclusions:

1. Patients who received deprenyl (alone or in
combination with tocopherol) reached a predetermined level of disability more slowly
than the patients who took tocopherol alone
or placebo. The results translate into a delay
in the development of disability of nearly one
year and an extended capacity for full-time
employment.

2. Deprenyl also produced slight short-term
benefits in alleviating symptoms.

3. Adverse effects were negligible.

4. Patients to whom deprenyl was administered had a significant delay in the development of disability severe enough to require
levodopa therapy.

These were the primary, clinical effects of deprenyl. Still to be answered was the intriguing question of deprenyl's "mechanism" — was it symptomatic, protective, or both?

The DATATOP authors confessed they did not yet know the answer. But they put forth a number of possibilities. One was that deprenyl "could have" exerted an effect on symptoms by increasing the availability of dopamine by inhibiting the action of the MAO enzyme. Other studies had indicated that deprenyl, without levodopa, did not relieve symptoms, but the DATATOP investigators were not prepared to dismiss this possibility.

"It is possible," the DATATOP investigators asserted, "that deprenyl may have produced symptomatic effects through its amphetamine and methamphetamine metabolities. Although [it has been] demonstrated that the effects of deprenyl in patients treated with levodopa do not depend on the pharmacologic properties of its amphetamine metabolities, clinically relevant amphetamine-like effects may occur in patients not treated with levodopa, such as those enrolled in our study."

The DATATOP authors were inclined to give little weight to the argument that the mechanism of deprenyl was related to its antidepressant properties. "Even patients with mild depression were excluded from [our] study . . . and the dosage of deprenyl [10 milligrams per day] has not been shown to produce antidepressant effects in patients with depression who do not have Parkinson's disease . . . Deprenyl may still have produced a general improvement, even if we could not detect it, in our patients' sense of well-being, similar to that observed in patients with Alzheimer's disease who were treated with deprenyl."

DATATOP has still not explained the *primary* effects of deprenyl. The most enticing possibility is that deprenyl protects brain cells from aging: ". . . we cannot be certain that deprenyl is exerting a truly protective effect over the long term. However, nothing in our data is inconsistent with this interpretation."

What DATATOP has proven beyond a doubt is that deprenyl postpones disability, significantly increases the length of time victims of Parkinson's may continue to be gainfully employed, increases productivity, and improves the quality of life.[3]

Although the DATATOP scientists have yet to publish any further data on the clinical progress of the patients in the study (which was due in the summer of 1992), one of them, Dr. P. A. LeWitt of the Wayne State University School of Medicine in Detroit, recently published a report which includes some additional findings from the study (*Acta Neurologica Scandivavica* - Supplementum, No. 136, 84:79-85, 1991).

Among the findings published by Dr. LeWitt are the following:

1. After 2 years of treatment with deprenyl, the risk of reaching the point at which L-Dopa treatment was needed because of the deterioration of the patient was reduced from a probability of 0.66 to 0.46;

2. Patients receiving deprenyl scored significantly higher in tests to evaluate the clinical

---

[3] Architects of the DATATOP study claim there is only one chance in a hundred million that their major finding — deprenyl delays the need for levodopa therapy — could have been a result of accident or chance.

status of the patients. Patients taking placebo showed a greater decline on rating scales such as the Hoehn and Yahr Rating Scale and the Schwab and England Clinical Disability Rating Scale than patients taking deprenyl.

Another study by Dr. J. O. Rinne of the University of Turku in Finland (*Acta Neurologica Scandinavica* - No. 136, 84:87-90, 1991) generated evidence that deprenyl treatment protects neurons (in the substantia nigra region of the brain) in Parkinson's disease patients. Dr. Rhine counted nigral neurons (upon autopsy) in the brains of patients who had been given deprenyl in addition to L-Dopa as well as in patients who had received only L-Dopa. He found that the number of neurons was significantly greater in patients who had received deprenyl in combination with L-Dopa than in patients who had received only L-Dopa, and concluded that deprenyl treatment "may retard the death" of nigral neurons.

Dr. LeWitt speculates on the possible mechanisms of action of deprenyl in protecting neurons in Parkinson's patients. Since small quantities of ampehtamine and l-methamphetamine are derived from the metabolism of deprenyl, he suggests the possibility that chronic exposure to these metabolites might produce changes in dopamine turnover or dopamine receptor function.

Another possibility discussed by Dr. LeWitt to explain deprenyl's clinical benefits in Parkinson's patients is through the action of 2-phenylethylamine (2-PE), which is increased substantially when MAO-B is inhibited by deprenyl. 2-PE is a "neuromodulator" which acts directly upon dopamine receptors and can produce behavioral effects similar to dopamine.

Another possible mechanism of action for deprenyl discussed by Dr. LeWitt is the stimulation of brain activity of superoxide dismustase (SOD), which counteracts the damaging effects of the superoxide radical produced during the degradation of dopamine by MAO-B. He also discusses evidence that deprenyl may be able to inhibit hydrogen peroxide radicals, which are produced as a result of dopamine metabolism. Since vitamin E is a scavenger of hydrogen peroxide radicals, it will be interesting to see the final findings of the DATATOP study regarding the effects of vitamin E on Parkinsonism.

The DATATOP Study has been of great interest because it is a multi-center trial in the United States and Canada conducted by dozens of first-rate scientists, in which the role of deprenyl in slowing the progression of Parkinson's disease is being investigated in hundreds of patients. The remarkable preliminary findings of the DATATOP study led to a 3-month randomized, double-blind multi-center trial of deprenyl in mildly-impaired Parkinson's patients in France, the initial finds of which have confirmed the DATATOP findings. In the French study, 18.4% of the patients taking placebo required L-Dopa treatment by the end of the trial, compared to only 4.5% of the patients taking deprenyl. A multi-center trial is currently underway in Italy, in which the effects of deprenyl in Parkinson's patients is being compared to patients receiving other anti-Parkinson's drugs (L-Dopa, bromocriptine, and lisuride). Suffice to say the benefits of deprenyl are so impressive, the researchers could not deny it to their control groups and they therefore both modified and extended this massive scientific study.

12

THE SEX DRIVE
QUESTION

DOES DEPRENYL HEIGHTEN human sexual desire?

This is the most provocative of questions, because the effect of drugs on sexual behavior does not easily lend itself to clinical inspection. There are no standards, there could be no "control" group against which to measure performance or satisfaction, and neither inference nor objective third-party observation can provide a definitive, scientific answer. But deprenyl *does* increase the libido.

The evidence for deprenyl?

• After centuries of debate, sexual desire is recognized to be not so much visceral as cerebral. (Visceral responses are generated by novelty, discrepancy and interruption, while the cerebral cognitive system interprets the world as threatening, elating, frightening, or joyful.) Deprenyl effects those cerebral processes identified with excitation of the senses.

• Emotions (of which sexual desire is the most powerful) are understood to be characteristics of an active, searching and thinking creature. Deprenyl supports the physiology of one of the activation centers of the brain.

• One of the metabolites of deprenyl is a psychostimulant. The general effect of psychostimulants is an elevation of mood.

• Deprenyl has been clinically proven to ameliorate the symptoms of depression and anxiety — the two mood conditions that are antithetical to sexual desire and arousal.

• Deprenyl has been shown to awaken the urge in sexually sluggish rats. Rats are not perfect models from which to predict human behavior, but — rat brains are similar to human brains in terms of their organization and biochemistry. As well, rats are simple creatures which are not subject to the complex cultural conditioning that affects the behavior of humans. Their *instinctive* responses therefore may be measured in relative isolation from the societal or environmental influences that affect humans.

• There is the empirical evidence. This is a body of evidence that cannot be measured because it is largely, although not entirely, anecdotal. It cannot be documented, with names, because it intrudes on the most private dimension of our being. The following two testimonials from an artist and a businessman, are necessarily anonymous:

"To be honest, I'm not sure of what this medication will mean in the long run; more
important to me has been the psychological
lift which I have experienced after taking
it . . ."

and,

"I again want to tell you what a magical effect
Eldepryl (deprenyl) has had on me. Eldepryl
has, I feel, released me from a cage . . ."

Until recently, sex was mankind's greatest myth. The
interest of medical science was confined to the processes connected with birth and the diseases associated
with sexual activity. The advent of the birth control pill
encouraged the study of sex as a means of pleasure
and fulfillment as well as the means of procreation.
When psychologists, and afterwards sociologists, began to address the subject of sex, they raised questions
as to the physiological and anatomical structures and
changes which might explain sexual function. Inexor-
ably, the trail backwards to the source of sexual desire
led to the brain.

But does the sex urge begin in the brain, or is the
brain simply an intermediary in the chain of events
and circumstances that lead to arousal?

Pavlov's view had been that behavioral processes
are conceived as events resulting from stimuli which
impinge on the organism without any previous activity in the behavioral field. But investigations through
the early part of this century have led to a more inte-
grative view — that while the desire for sex may come
from an external stimulus, there is an active reflex in

the brain that triggers response and might even be the well-spring for sexual arousal.

Finding the source of any emotion — sexual desire being among the most primitive of emotions — is a problem that bedevils brain scientists. Well into this century, the prevailing philosophical speculation was that emotions were disturbances of, or interferences with, rational behavior.

In recent years, as the brain began to yield to rough outlines of its anatomy, attempts have been made to associate various aspects of behavior with specific parts of the brain. With these attempts has come an almost random search to localize the source of sexual desire. Was it in the brainstem? The midbrain? The limbic system? The hippocampus? All of these brain systems play a role in sexual function for the simple reason that sex encompasses not only learning and experience and environmental influences but also tactile and olfactory and auditory sensations.

Passive research has stumbled over the fact that brain abnormalities may be associated with unusual sexual behavior. Epileptics suffering from disturbances in their temporal lobes have been observed in displays of fetishism; and studies of male transvestites or transsexuals have turned up an unusual proportion of abnormal electroencephalograms (EEGs). In West Germany, men convicted of paedophilia have shown less inclination to aberrant sexual behavior after having part of the hypothalamus removed.

Although it is now recognized that brain chemistry accounts for sexual performance and that chemicals secreted within the brain affect every function, medical science continues to be chary on the subject of drugs and sexuality.

As a substance which affects brain function, deprenyl has always been talked about as a drug "with a peculiar pharmacological spectrum." In layman's language, deprenyl seemed to do a lot of things differently than any other drug. The term *peculiar pharmacological spectrum* also suggests that deprenyl does a number of different things and has a number of different effects.

From the time Joseph Knoll called the drug "a new spectrum psychic energizer" in 1964, there has been a fascination about deprenyl's family relationship to amphetamines. Knoll himself had identified amphetamine as one of the metabolites of deprenyl, meaning that amphetamine was one of the intermediary byproducts of the metabolism of deprenyl.

Knoll felt that the amphetamine produced as a byproduct in the brain was not harmful or addictive. It was a less pharmacologically active form of amphetamine. Animal studies have supported this opinion. In chronic toxicity studies performed with rats and dogs, there was no evidence of withdrawal symptoms to indicate the kind of dependency popularly associated with amphetamine. And, deprenyl's use by millions of people over the past 15 to 20 years empirically confirms Dr. Knoll's research.

There is a reference to increased libido in the first U.S. clinical trial that sought to measure deprenyl's antidepressant activity. In a group of 12 endogenously depressed patients, eight females and four males, deprenyl produced a significant improvement over the whole range of depressive symptomatology.

According to the authors of the study, "of particular interest" was the improvement in levels of anxiety. Although side effects from the use of deprenyl were minimal, one of the most common was increased libido.[1]

Does deprenyl increase sex drive simply because it makes people feel better? Or does it heighten libido more specifically because of its antidepressant range of effects? Or — does it incline people toward arousal because the brain's dopaminergic system, which deprenyl supports, is important to sexual function?

Professor Merton Sandler of the Queen Charlotte Hospital points to a body of experimental evidence showing the importance of dopamine in sexual function. Back in 1972, Sandler had reviewed some of the reported side effects of levodopa (which is metabolized to dopamine in the brain). He says, "One facet of treatment with levodopa that became notorious, receiving much publicity in the lay press, was its putative aphrodisiac effect."[2]

London's Fleet Street newspapers took particular relish in reporting this side effect of levodopa. The headlines included A WONDER DRUG MAKES A SICK OLD MAN START CHASING NURSES and 'SEX DRUG' MADE A MAN OF 60 CHASE HIS NURSES.

Sandler was at first inclined to believe that effects of this type were merely a by-product of increased physical well-being. Other scientists made different observations. A Dutch doctor reported the case of an 88-year-old female patient with senile dementia, without

---

[1] "Deprenyl: A Selective Monoamine Oxidase Type-B inhibitor in Endogenous Depression," Mann, John and Gershon, Samuel, *Life Sciences* Vol 26, 877-82 (Pergammon Press, 1980).

---

[2] Sandler's observations on the importance of dopamine in sexual function were reported in "Catecholamine Synthesis and Metabolism in Man: Clinical Implications, with Special Reference to Parkinsonism," *Handbook of Experimental Pharmacology*, Vol 23 (Springer-Verlag, 1972).

physical impairment, in whom treatment with levodopa was followed by an intense preoccupation with
sex. Andre Barbeau, the Montreal neurologist, had observed a number of cases where levodopa increased
arousal. (Others pointed out that dopamine, apart
from its actions in the central nervous system, was the
predominant amine in the penis.)

In Psychopharmacology: The Third Generation of
Progress,[3] Cort A. Pederson and Arthur J. Prange, Jr.
drew attention to the fact that "dopamine neurotrans-
mission appears to play an important part in penile
erection and ejaculation independent of its facilitating
role in copulatory behavior."

Sex is unlike any other behavior in that it does not
result from a desire to navigate between the guide-
posts of pain and pleasure. It is, by itself, a drive,
surpassed in its intensity only by the desire to survive.

Joseph Knoll's thesis is that, among the compartments of the brain, the dopaminergic system is an "ex-
citatory" system that determines whether an animal
"will be ready to surmount every obstacle, even if life
is in the balance, to seize its food or reach its sexual
partner." Knoll's experiment with rats showed him
that (a) animals that were more sexually active were
better learners, and (b) more active animals live significantly longer.

Deprenyl, which is highly selective in its effects on
the dopaminergic system of the brain, awakened the
sexual urge in rats and extended their lifespan. But not
all rats responded in the same fashion. There were ex-
treme variations in sexual performance, which led
Knoll to examine human experience and conclude:
"Exactly the same correlations were found in our
studies with male rats."

We cannot conduct a clinical trial to measure the effects of deprenyl on sexuality of humans because — to mention just one obstacle — how would we select the "controls"? We may roughly compare our own sex drive, today, with what we thought it was last week or last year. But in every other respect, sex defies comparison.

Deprenyl's effect on the libido may be measured only according to (a) inferences made from "soft" data on what people say and how they behave, (b) our understanding of the brain and the way it transmits the messages that are translated into our behavior. That the dopaminergic system regulates human "drive" is supported by empirical evidence that this brain system is important to efficient physical and mental functioning.

Will deprenyl increase your sex drive? The only way to answer this question is to say — try it. Deprenyl's side effects are few and its benefits to overall health are many. You have nothing to lose and everything to gain.

13

THE FOUNTAIN OF YOUTH?

THE FETCHING NOTION that a drug can help mankind live longer and healthier lives seems far off in the future. There is not one drug, however, that is sold because of claims that it prolongs life.[1] While modern medicine maybe increasingly preoccupied with all kinds of treatments, including drugs, that improve the quality of life in later years, the extension of life span by pharmaceutical means has remained in the realm of science fiction, until now.

Joseph Knoll makes an engaging argument that deprenyl is capable of extending life span. Knoll starts from the proposition that aging is a physiological phenomenon. He concedes that there are myriad changes that lead to physiological aging and that most of these changes, which occur at the molecular level, have as yet gone undetected.

---

[1] The U.S. Food and Drug Administration forbids any claims that a drug may have life-prolonging effects.

One of the first age-related biochemical changes in the body's physiology was discovered in 1961 by Oleh Hornykiewicz when he found that the chemical transmitter dopamine was absent in the postmortem brains of Parkinson's victims.

Knoll says, "The age-related progressive decline of dopaminergic control in the brain seems to be the first firmly established biochemical lesion of aging." He points to studies that have demonstrated that the loss of dopamine is accompanied by, and in all probability caused by, the increased activity of the MAO enzyme.

MAO is found in heightened concentrations in the brains of older people. High concentrations of MAO in the brain are the one common pathological link between Parkinson's disease and Alzheimer's. "The unequivocal conclusion," Knoll says, "is that MAO activity in the brain increases selectively with advanced age, and the age-dependent increase in MAO activity is due entirely to higher enzyme concentration in brain tissue." Knoll verified this conclusion using rats. His "tool" was deprenyl, the drug that inhibits the activity of the MAO enzyme.

Animal aging experiments are generally conducted with rats, mice, and hamsters. They are the most convenient laboratory species, in part because they have life spans of only two to three years. Furthermore, all rodents are members of the same class of vertebrates as humans and possess many of the same characteristics. They are adaptable: they can live comfortably in different kinds of habitats and can flourish on a wide variety of diets. Of the 1,500 species of rodents, rats in particular are persistent creatures. They are active and like to explore, characteristics that make them good subjects for scientific observation.

The central nervous system of rats works much the same way as that of humans. Although the higher portion of a rat brain is less developed than that of humans, it has all the same elements as a human brain — the structure, cells, and chemistry are the same.

Some scientists say that experimental studies with animals have little meaningful significance for man and cannot be the basis for generalization, largely because animals are "species specific" and the results of studies may not be duplicated in humans. Nevertheless, experiments on rats and other animals are responsible for many advances in the understanding of nerve impulses in the brain, the mapping of the brain's pathways, and the concepts of its functional circuits.

Knoll began by selecting 132 male albino rats, all the same age and all sexually inexperienced. During their twenty-fourth month (the maximum age of most strains of rats is approximately 45 months), the rats were given weekly mating tests. Of the 132 rats, 46 "failed" altogether — they didn't mount, they didn't intromit (penetrate), and they didn't ejaculate. This was the "noncopulatory" category. A further group of 44 rats mounted and intromitted during testing (the "sluggish" category), and the remaining 42 did not go beyond mounting. Each of these three "activity" categories was divided by two, resulting in two groups of 66 rats each.

All of the rats were to inhabit the same environment and all were to be given the same strictly controlled diet. Half were administered periodic doses of an innocent saline solution. The other half were given deprenyl instead of the saline solution.

Of the control group — the "saline rats" — none became sexually active in that they achieved ejaculation. The number of those who accomplished intromission, or even just mounting, declined steadily. Of the other group — the "deprenyl group" — 10 of the 66 became sexually active within a month and, by the end of the eighth month, 24 were sexually active. In the first few months of testing, others among the deprenyl group showed a growing inclination to mount, and to intromit, before their faculties began to decline.

There was a marked correlation between sexual interest and life span: the tendency in both groups of rats was for longevity to increase in proportion to degree of sexual activity. The most striking result was that the average lifespan of the 66 rats whose diet included deprenyl was 49.5 months. This was well beyond the 45.5 months that had previously been observed as the maximum age of a rat.

The first member of the saline group to die was 35 months old. The last remaining member of this control group survived to be 39 months. In contrast, the *first* of the deprenyl group to die was almost 43 months. This was older than the longest lived of the saline group. The last of the deprenyl group to die was 54 months — 8.5 months longer than the supposed maximum life span of a rat.

In a postscript to the rat study, Knoll wrote:

> My suggestion is that the basic difference between individuals is in their ability to generate that kind of specific activation of the brain which determines the efficiency of their drive-motivated behavior. The intensity of the drives determines the time spent with purposeful activity and, as a result, deter-

mines the chances to reach the goals giving satisfaction. This ability seems to have a decisive influence on the aging of the brain and of life span. According to this working hypothesis, the more intensive are the drives, the slower is the mental decay and the longer is the span of life. The nigrostriatal dopaminergic machinery seems to be one of the very few brain mechanisms which control the drives, i.e., determine the efficiency of drive-motivated behavior.

A sophisticated and safe complex medication which keeps the whole catecholaminergic

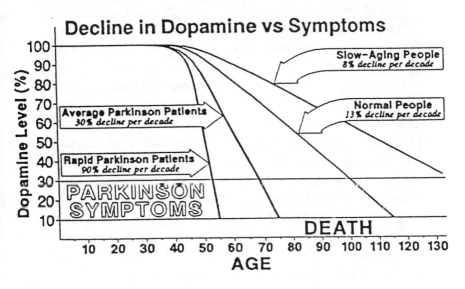

As the above chart illustrates, we begin to lose dopamine producing cells in our 40's. Some researchers ascribe this loss to the "free radical theory of aging" — but — irrespective of theory, the loss is a fact. A fact that can only be circumvented by the use of deprenyl to protect the dopamine producing cells of the brain.

brain system a high-activity level and protects it from aging may offer new chances for fighting against the age-dependent mental decay and may also substantially decrease the incidence of age-related mental disease.

To follow the path opened up by deprenyl-induced longevity of male rats is compelling, because to improve quality of life in senescence is beyond all question the highest priority project in a rapidly aging society.

Knoll's paper was published in New York's *Mount Sinai Medical Journal* in January 1988.

"What did she die from?"

The answer, with a fatalistic shrug, "Old age."

Simple as that. The time clock just ran out. For generations we have accepted this as an indisputable biological fact.

The aging process — the process that has its final resolution in death — is not within our control. Or is it? Joseph Knoll believes it is. He believes he has found in a tiny portion of the brain the mechanism that can slow the aging process and, maybe, even extend our life spans. At the very least Knoll believes he has found a drug that manipulates this brain mechanism in such a way that we can better enjoy the last years of our lives.

Prior to the 1950s most studies on aging were made on residents of nursing homes and other long-term health care facilities. But the fact that these subjects often suffered from one or more chronic ailments and took numerous medications made it difficult to identify the true effects (and therefore causes) of aging. In 1958 the Gerontology Center of the National Institute of Aging in Baltimore began investigating the aging process in normal, healthy males. There were some surprising findings: one was that the heart does not fail as a person ages. And if it does fail, the cause is probably disease and not aging. Overall, the results proved that aging and disease are not synonymous.

The question raised by that conclusion was, then, what causes aging?

Today gerontologists, neurologists, pharmacologists, and other scientists are chipping away at the maxim that three score years and ten constitutes a natural and acceptable human life span.

Although aging and growing old may be different things, scientists are searching for the keys to the most insidious of all life's processes. Survey after survey has revealed that the greatest fear of people beyond adolescence is aging. Not going bankrupt, not being bereaved, not suffering a crippling accident, but aging. The onslaught of failing eye sight, stiffening joints, aching back, eardrums that fail to resonate the way they once did, all of these are worrisome. Or there may be thumping chest pains, troubled sleep, memory lapses, the alarming onset of diminished sexual interest, wrinkles, and, small wonder, bouts of depression. The fear is not merely predicated on growing old, but also on becoming a burden to others.

These are the unmistakable signs of growing old. Unmistakable, surely. But inevitable? Maybe not. Over the past decade scientists have been edging closer to the conclusion that the whole process of aging may be significantly retarded if already under way, and substantially postponed if it has not already begun in earnest. They have reached this point by asking two questions. Why *do* we age? And why do we die because of it?

Joseph Knoll's thesis is:

> Aging, the unfortunate common fate of all mature adults, is a physiological phenomenon. It essentially means the decadence of the quality of life with the passage of time. The easily recognizable outside appearances of aging (graying hair, wrinkling skin, need of glasses for reading, etc.) give some information about the chronological age of the person. But these signs are not necessarily in complete harmony with the physiological age of the organ systems, with the measurable decrements of integrated functions, and with the almost unmeasurable mental deterioration.

He adds, not without hope: "The exact measurement of the age-related changes in man remain difficult because the most reliable technique — to follow the changes in the same person over the entire age span — is practically unfeasible."

Hence, Dr. Knoll's experiments with rats, which previously were believed to have a maximum technical life span (TLS) of 182 weeks, and his startling discovery that dosages of deprenyl not only postponed symptoms of aging, but actually prolong the life span of rats beyond the previously accepted maximum.

"This," he claimed, "is the first instance that by the aid of a well-aimed medication members of a species lived beyond the known life span maximum." The simplicity of that statement, and the scant recognition outside a narrow segment of the scientific community, could belie the monumental implication this discovery may hold for the human race.

For the first time, someone is saying we do not have to grow old. Will Knoll's name be etched on one of the great milestones in human evolution?

It is in the twentieth century that revolutionary advances have dramatically increased life expectancy. In the developed countries of the industrial world, the proportion of population more than 65 years old is today five times greater than it was 100 years ago. The average life expectancy in the United States at the turn of the century was 47 years. Today the average white American male may expect to reach his three score years and ten, with females attaining 77, for a mean average of 73.

This in itself represents an extraordinary achievement, but lurking behind these impressive statistics is the fact that one of medical science's major impacts on old age has been to ensure that more of us reach it. As Dr. James F. Fries has pointed out in the *New England Journal of Medicine:*

> A more critical look at [the] data demonstrates that they reflect progress in the elimination of premature death, particularly neonatal mortality. For persons 40 years of age and older, life expectancy has increased relatively little; for those 75 years old the increase is barely perceptible.[2]

---

[2]James F. Fries, "Aging, Natural Death, and the Compression of Morbidity," *New England Journal of Medicine* (July 1980).

In other words, once we reach 75, our chances of living longer are not much greater than they were at the beginning of the century.

Fries's studies at the Stanford University Medical Center led him to conclude that as we complete the process of eliminating most disease ("acute diseases"), our mean age at death should be "not far from 85 years." With ravaging fatal diseases such as smallpox, tuberculosis, and poliomyelitis virtually eradicated in the United States and Canada, dramatic progress has been made in expanding life expectancy. These acute diseases, therefore, have now been replaced as the major cause of death by "chronic" diseases associated with aging. All of these — including arteriosclerosis, arthritis, cancer, and cirrhosis — are believed to commence early in life, often undetected, until they wreak a havoc of disease and disability later on.

Fries concludes: "Clearly the medical and social task of eliminating premature death is largely accomplished. Acute illness has ceased to be the major medical problem in the United States." The Fries thesis, first published in 1980, advocates a dramatic shift in medical efforts to what he terms "postponement rather than cure." His goal, then, has been to focus on "morbidity" — that is, the nature or indications of disease — rather than mortality.

Fries's strategy would see the vast majority of people living full, active lives unimpaired by disease or disability well into their eighties, whereupon they would die without lingering, undue illness. As Fries puts it: "A radically different view of the life span and of society, in which life is physically, emotionally, and intellectually vigorous until shortly before its close, when like the marvelous 'one-hoss shay,' everything comes apart at once and repair is impossible. Such a life approaches the intuitive ideal of many and confounds the dread of others for the opposite model, that of ever more lingering death

But is the Friesian 85 years an accurate estimate of our maximum life span? Approximately one human in 10,000 in the developed countries of the world actually beats this figure by 15 years to reach the age of one century. The *Guinness Book of World Records* documents the singularly most authenticated individual age in the world as a Japanese fisherman who lived to be 120.

Fries himself notes these examples of human antiquity and concedes that the human life span may indeed not be fixed.

Perhaps the only problem for many of us living now is that we will not know the answer in our lifetimes. It would take too long to find out. Hence the landmark rat experiment, showing that deprenyl extended the maximum technical life span for rats. The significance for humans of these rat experiments is not known. But there is evidence that deprenyl helps people with Parkinson's disease to live longer.

But whether or not deprenyl is capable of prolonging the human life span, that is another question. Is deprenyl capable of "improving the quality of life in senescence?" If this is the case, and evidence is accumulating, deprenyl is the first of a family of drugs that will make life worthwhile in our penultimate years.

Knoll is not the only scientist who believes that the human life span may be extended. He is joined by, among others, Professor Leonard Hayflick, director of the University of Florida's Center for Gerontological Studies.

No single theory offers the complete answer to

aging; many of these theories are not mutually exclusive, and none precludes the possibility that some dramatic new discovery may render them obsolete. However, all of these theories offer fascinating insights into the mysteries of the aging process. The traditional belief has been that the organs of the body and the brain itself have a finite chemical life span. James Fries puts a new twist on this theory:

> An important shift is occurring in the conceptualization of the chronic disease and of aging. Premature organ dysfunction, whether of muscle, heart, lung, or joint, is beginning to be conceived as stemming from disuse of the faculty, not overuse. At the Stanford Arthritis Clinic I tell patients to exercise and to "use it or lose it." For example, the new advice of the cardiologist is "run, not rest."

The body, to an increasing degree, is now felt to rust out rather than wear out. These processes involve oxygen, commonly known to us as a prerequisite of life itself, and radiation, the postwar nuclear age synonym for death itself. While no animal or plant life can survive without oxygen, any organism exposed to too much of it will be severely damaged, or even destroyed, by its toxic effects.

This fact leads us to the free radical theory of aging, postulated by Dr. Denham Harman of the American Aging Association, Inc., at the University of Nebraska Medical Center. A free radical is an unstable molecule or atom because it has an unpaired electron. Picture it as running around in our brains and bodies, lustfully pairing with other stable molecules and causing all kinds of problems by setting off chemical reactions that are sometimes deadly.[3] Some free radicals are a natural intermediate product in the metabolism of foods and other chemicals, and our bodies produce the proteins known as enzymes to supervise them. It is when these free radicals get out of control that Dr. Harman says we are in trouble.

One of the chemical reactions caused by free radicals is the oxidation of polyunsaturated fatty acids, but any cell in the human body is vulnerable. Lipofuscin, for example, also affects the substantia nigra, the part of our central nervous system that produces dopamine. But what is lipofuscin? We know it as "liver spots," the telltale brown blotches that appear on our skin with the arrival of old age. Lipofuscin is, in fact, a waste product of the body's chemistry, deposited not only in the wrinkled old hands of the elderly, but also in vital organs such as the heart and liver — and in the brain, where it is believed lipofuscin blocks off the supply of nutrients to brain cells. The chemical mischief of free radicals is believed to be one of the causes of cardio-vascular disease, arthritis, and cancer, as well as a root cause of aging. The free radicals our bodies produce by chemical reactions are, in fact, a minor duplication of the effects we experience upon exposure to radiation. They play a role in the degenerative diseases of the central nervous system and impair the functions of our bodies' immune systems.

"The aging process," says Dr. Harman, "may simply be the sum of the deleterious free radical reaction going on continuously through our cells and tissues . . . spontaneous mutation, cancer, and aging can be

---

[3]Pearson, Durk and Shaw, Sandy, *Life Extension: A Practical Scientific Approach* (New York: Warner, 1982).

looked upon as a result of the continuous 'internal radiation' while these same processes produced by external radiation are largely the result of an increment in the amount of total 'radiation' to which the body is exposed."

So what can be done about free radicals? It has been demonstrated that the aging effects of free radicals — the oxidizing or rusting-up — can be counteracted by feeding laboratory animals antioxidants that inhibit the process. Mice, rats, and fruitflies have all lived longer when fed antioxidants. In these instances, however, none of these creatures has exceeded its maximum life expectancy.

(Joseph Knoll's deprenyl compound is a form of antioxidant. What distinguishes it from others is that it has *specific* properties and only does the job it is supposed to do — it affects those cells whose behavior it is targeted to modify. Its tendency to ignore, for the most part, other cells in the body makes it a "clean" drug with minimal side effects.)

In reviewing Dr. Harman's studies, Leonard Hayflick noted: "The experimental data suggest that administration of free radical antagonists, such as antioxidants, increase life *expectation* [author's emphasis] substantially. Nevertheless, factors that tend to increase life expectation do not necessarily play a role in the aging process."

Hayflick concluded that: "The amelioration of some or all of these diseases or causes of death by antioxidants simply increases life expectations, not life span. It is probable that only by increasing life span, or maximum age of death, of members of a species, will important insights be made into the aging process."

This conclusion, of course, is precisely the accomplishment of Joseph Knoll in his laboratory experiments on rats fed deprenyl. His experiments, which have been replicated in Canada and are being studied in the United States, increased the maximum life span of a *species*.[4]

Knoll is concerned with the broad physiological theories of aging. The *immunological theory of aging* centers on the immune system. In the past few years millions of people around the world have acquired at least a rudimentary knowledge of the body's immune system through the tragic epidemic of AIDS, the sexually transmitted disease that destroys our natural ability to fight off life-threatening viruses and the bacteria that constantly invade our systems. AIDS destroys this defense force of immunity and we die prematurely.

Our immune system is a veritable army of disease-fighting cells and antibodies controlled by the thymus gland, which acts as a control center for their activity. At the direction of the thymus, white blood cells known as T-cells, rush to kill off the body's poisonous invaders and also manufacture antibodies to do the same thing.

The problem and the connection of the immune system with the aging process lies in the fact that the thymus gland reaches its peak performance in a humans' teenage years and thereafter commences a qualitative and quantitative decline. In old age its performance is no more than five to ten percent of the

---

[4]"Deprenyl Prolongs Survival of Aged Rats," Ivey, G. O., Racine, R. J., Ellis, P., Mendonca, A., and Milgram, N. W., *Life Sciences*, University of Toronto. "Our results . . . indicated that deprenyl can prolong the survival of laboratory rats even when treatment is begun at a late age."

efficiency it displayed around the time of puberty. Thus, from a very early age, our ability to defend ourselves against invading disease is constantly reduced.

Exactly why the immune system deteriorates is not known. What is known is that the release of growth hormone by the brain also declines after puberty, affecting the thymus gland, which depends on the hormone for efficient performance. Some theorists have extrapolated this fact into the suggestion that since thymic atrophy can act as a kind of trigger for the aging process, it may well be a master chronometer for growing old.

How ironic it is that as we grow older and more susceptible to disease and infection, the very system devised to defend us becomes less and less capable of doing so — even to the point where its mistakes can seriously aggravate the condition it was once capable of destroying. Such thoughts lead us to the possibility that this process is no accident, and that death and the aging process itself are controlled by some predetermined schedule. Conditioned as we are to measure our lives in units of time — days, weeks, years — it takes no great leap of imagination to theorize that our very life span may be governed by a series of preset time clocks of which the immune system is just one. There is growing evidence that this may, in fact, prove to be the case, which is why today's gerontologists are considering ways to reset the clock, if not make it tick beyond the witching hour. It is this prospect that leads to the *neuroendocrine theory of aging.*

Leonard Hayflick grew cultured human connective tissue cells and discovered that they only replicated themselves approximately 50 times.[5] He theorized that the cells themselves had a built-in life span or time clock that would ring at its appointed hour and thus prevent the growth and replenishment of the body. It is this time clock concept that is at the root of the neuroendocrine theory of aging. It involves the endocrine system, which produces hormones essential to the functioning of some of the body's critical organs, including the sexual, reproductive capability. As well, it involves the body's central nervous system, which, through a combination of electrical and chemical changes, controls actions and responses throughout the body.

Both systems — the endocrine and central nervous system — degenerate with age, and no part of the body can escape the consequences of their degeneration. When such critical components as hormone production units and the neurotransmitters of the brain — the brain's message-carrying network — are in decline, how can the whole system not begin to lose equilibrium and collapse toward death? Proponents of the neuroendocrinal theory of aging argue that it cannot.

Scientists have discovered that if the pituitary gland is removed from salmon, spawning is prevented and the fish survive for several years past their normal life span. With the pituitary removed, there is no release of the oxidizing hormone that kills them after spawning. The time clock, in effect, has been turned off.

So, is there a correlation between salmon and man?

---

[5]Contrary to the Hayflick constant that human cellular division is limited to approximately 50 replications, modern biochemical intervention has allowed the extension of cellular replication in all cultures to well over 70 times, which in terms of human lifespan equates to a minimum of 140 years and a maximum of 490 years, as most cells have a 2 to 7 year cycle of replication.

Hayflick says: "The survival of a species does not depend on its members surviving much beyond the age of sexual maturation. From the standpoint of evolution, there is no survival value for our species to have a life expectation much beyond the reproductive years." That may be so, "from the standpoint of evolution," but man is a particular species, separated from all other species by his ability to reason.

Joseph Knoll, he of the catholicity of interests, the scientist who has made his mission to "improve the quality of life in senescence," believes in the force of nature. He understands that nature cannot be changed. He does believe, however, that "what is given by nature we can either enhance or inhibit."

Knoll's mind ranges so far and wide that he is not persuaded by any particular theory of aging. He accepts the fact that our genetic system — itself and the environment in which it operates — influences our longevity. He fully understands the third law of thermodynamics, which brings the inevitability of bone deterioration as we progress through the postdevelopmental years of our lives. Beyond those two factors, he believes that the aging process is influenced by some inner "drive" that has its headquarters in the brain.

While Knoll believes that deprenyl is a pharmaceutical that will elevate the dignity of human beings in their twilight years, the drug by itself cannot be the answer to the mystery of aging and longevity. "Deprenyl is a highly important tool, but there must be a *system* for deprenyl to work within. We need to understand that system, that physiology."

He elaborated this notion in a speech at the University of Bologna, Italy, in April 1989: "The riddle to be solved is how the organism as a whole dies, if, although the passing of time deteriorates part of the system, the aged organs are fit for life even at the time of death . . . For the living beings with the highly refined organization, it is the brain which has the absolute priority in maintaining the sophisticated integration between the almost confusing systems of cells synchronizing them to a lucidly arranged and purposeful entity."

Knoll conceded that "the natural aging of each organ must have its meaning and adverse consequences for the individual [but] none of these individual organs can compare in significance with the central nervous system. Only the pace of age-related changes in the brain seems to me to be of rate-limiting importance in controlling the duration of life, as the brain secures how long an organism, as an integrated, ultrastable system, will definitely operate."

It was in the brain, Knoll said, that the critical time-clocks must be measuring out life span, communicating their death sentence through the very same message network used to maintain life. That network had been discovered by chemist Julius Axelrod of the U.S. National Institute of Mental Health, winner of the Nobel prize in 1970. Axelrod was the first to demonstrate how brain cells or neurons communicate with one another by releasing the chemical noradrenaline, which is related to catecholamines, of which dopamine is but one. All of these chemicals perform vital roles in regulating cardiovascular functions, movement, mood, and thought. In the highly nationalistic world of science, Axelrod was anointed, in the United States if not universally, the father of modern neuroscience.

From Axelrod's pioneering work on this chemical

transmission within the brain came the development of antidepressant drugs that would conserve the chemical messenger and help alleviate mental distress. It was little more than a coincidence that Knoll, years earlier, had developed deprenyl as an antidepressant, not then realizing what other properties deprenyl might turn out to have.

When Knoll began to scour the nooks and crannies of the brain more closely, he found the tiny segment known as the substantia nigra, where the message-carrying dopaminergic system was the brains' most rapidly aging component. What fascinated Knoll about the substantia nigra was not only its location at the center of this aging process, but also its function. The substantia nigra is the section of the brain that controls the very life force and survival instinct that enables man to continue the struggle for and enjoyment of life.

Knoll told his audience at the University of Bologna:

> The population of neurons [in the substantia nigra] transformed into a highly excitable state is, of course, different in the brain of an animal which is driven by hunger or by sexual desire or the fear of predators. There is, however, a common physicist mechanism for any type of drive. This is the catecholaminergic system in the brain. Though analogies are always false, I would compare the catecholaminergic brain system to the engine of a car which is permanently raced and always ready to bring the machine into motion if the driver depresses the pedal. The network of neurons in the state of specific activation pre-

sents the driver with the knowledge of the goal — that is, where to drive the car.

To continue Knoll's reluctant analogy to its conclusion.

The same group of neurons can direct the "car" to a restaurant to eat. They can send it speeding off to avoid some life-threatening collision, or down a leafy lane to some sexually seductive rendezvous, or off on a pleasant scenic drive. When there is a good deal of mileage on the car, however, the neurons can steer it right off a cliff to destruction.

Furthermore, Knoll told his audience:

It is a universal, intrinsic, inborn mechanism from which there is no escape and which reduces the function of the system with slow but irresistible progression. Because of the unique role of the catecholaminergic system in securing the animals' ability to adapt itself to the environment and to cope with dangerous situations, and because catecholamines are unparalleled in their ability to generate excessive amounts of toxic free radicals which must lead sooner or later to the functional decay of the system, we deal here with a built-in suicide mechanism.

Because the neurons with the catecholaminergic transmission — especially the dopaminergic neurons in the substantia nigra — represent the most rapidly aging system in the brain, the consequences are clear: the more time elapsed after reaching sexual maturity, the less intensive are the drives, the lower are the chances to hold on successfully in the never-ending, merciless competition for survival.

The working hypothesis can be formulated that the aging of the catecholaminergic brain system is the built-in mechanization which determines the postdevelopmental longevity of an individual and explains why under the brutal conditions of prehistoric times humans never lived longer than three decades. I am definitely suggesting that the span of life depends on the utmost tricky aging of the catecholaminergic brain system and its functional consequences.

The study of neurochemistry began in earnest only about two decades ago. It has been encouraged by the growing proportion of older people, a powerful motive force frequently characterized as the group that will have the greatest social and economic impact on the future of society. The study of neurochemistry, especially in older members of the population, has also been encouraged by the development of psychotherapeutic drugs, among which deprenyl has proven its importance.

There are many things one could say about deprenyl. Its amazing benefits for most people suffering from Parkinson's, Alzheimer's and other brain diseases; its benefits to the sexually dysfunctional and those suffering from depression — these benefits are easily demonstrated.

It is the prevention of these diseases and the extension of human life span that is difficult to prove even though indicated by all studies. However, as health conscious people throughout the world add deprenyl to their health regimen, 20 or 30 years from now we may see the result — vigorous, youthful 85 year-olds — and I plan to be one of them.

APPENDIX

APPENDIX

A

CASE STUDIES BY
DR. RONALD KLATZ

Our culture is so imbued with the thought of the senior years as a time of illness, infirmity and ultimately death, that it is hard for many people to understand that we literally are at the threshold of an entirely new age of medicine and science — the age of anti-aging medicine.

The new paradigm of health will be the elimination of the aging process as an inevitable and uncontrollable reality of dysfunction and deterioration. It will soon be possible for most, if not all persons alive and healthy in the next 25 years, to expect to be 40 something or younger, almost forever. We have seen life expectancy increase greatly in the USA from an average lifespan of 49 years in the year 1900 to just over 76 years lifespan today. In Japan, the average lifespan for women is exceeding 84 years, and this spiraling increase in longevity shows no sign of decreasing nor should we expect it to.

The green revolution of the 1960's used genetic con-

iotech molecular cloning techniques to de-
ie resistant high-yield crops which in many
...ipied grain output. In a similar way the human
biomedical revolution of the 1990's is now making
great strides in uncovering a new understanding of
cellular aging and neuroendocrine feedback mechanisms for the human organism, allowing us amazing
and unexpected ways of intervening in the basic mechanisms of human aging of which the ability of deprenyl to protect the vital dopamine system is a prime
example.

The following are just a glimpse at the improvement
which is possible today in both the quality and quan-
tity of the human lifespan, and are actual case histories
of patients helped with deprenyl and other life extension therapies now in use at the American Longevity
Research Institute in Chicago.

The near-term horizon promises many more powerful technologies. So if you're planning on an extraordi-
narily long and healthy life — congratulations — your
chances are better than ever and improving each day.

THE USE OF MEDICATIONS for other than their labeled
and intended or FDA-approved use is called off-label
prescribing. Although off-label prescribing is not recommended nor endorsed by the American Medical
Association nor the Food and Drug Administration, it
still (at least for now) remains within the choice and
the power of all physicians practicing within the USA.
Since the beginning of Western medicine it has been
the right and the duty of the doctor to prescribe any
medication or treatment that a physician believes to be
in his patient's best interest, no matter what the published indication or approved use may be. Such is the

case with Eldepryl, manufactured by Sommerset Pharmaceuticals and distributed by Sandoz. Eldepryl is a brand name for Deprenyl tablets.

At the American Longevity Research Institute in Chicago IL, numbers of people have requested that they be placed on this drug for reasons other than that they are afflicted with Parkinson's disease. Currently the only approved use of this substance is for those whose Parkinson's has proven unresponsive to L-Dopa. As a practicing physician, prescribing this Rx to my patients for off-label indications is to take serious risks with the potential for malpractice suits — not to mention potential loss of my license — should future unforeseen complications arise from the use of this medication.

Just the same, at ALRI we have found that the benefits of using this substance for indications other than Parkinson's disease significantly outweigh the potential risks. And so at our facility we have treated dozens of people with deprenyl since 1990 and we have had varying degrees of success. Most importantly, as of now no patients have experienced serious or dangerous side effects.

Founded in 1984, American Longevity Research Institute is a non-profit scientific organization dedicated to helping people achieve an ageless future of health and vitality by eliminating the infirmities associated with aging. The scientists and physicians at ALRI successfully prevent age-related diseases through early diagnosis, individualized physical fitness programs, nutrition/hormone profiles and by optimizing metabolic function.

What follows are four case histories collected from my ALRI medical practice. The patients are individuals who sought out our care after having tried traditional treatments that failed to alleviate their symptoms. In each case, after careful consultation, we decided that the best course of action would be to place them on deprenyl. Since putting these patients on this therapy, all have experienced extremely positive results.

Please realize that these four cases are only perhaps 5% of the individuals treated with deprenyl thus far and that they were chosen for their dynamic improvements. Others report moderate to no improvement. It seems that although deprenyl can work wonders in some, nothing works wonders in all clients, save diet, nutrition, caring, and emotional support. Another limitation of this method of anecdotal reporting is that the results are not confirmed by controls using non-active placebos. Also, all the subjects received specific nutritional support tailored to their individual needs in addition to taking deprenyl. Even so, each of these individuals was receiving nutrition and fitness advice for many months prior to beginning deprenyl therapy.

I am convinced from personal observation that these four cases are a fair and realistic representation of the benefits some individuals can receive via the use of deprenyl in addition to a comprehensive nutritional program designed to maximize personal health and fitness.

Subject 1

Chad was a 39-year-old male businessman who was experiencing complaints of unexplained fatigue (excessive need for sleep despite taking frequent naps, and an overall feeling of tiredness), diminished sexual interests, and also a hint of depression. Because of his fatigue Chad was irritable and hence, unable to keep up with his normal social contacts. He had stopped going out on weekends and was beginning to have trouble getting himself to go to work in the morning. He had been to several doctors, all of whom had told him that it was "all in his head." By the time he arrived at ALRI, he had little hope of ever getting better.

We immediately gave him a thorough physical, but the lab findings were all within normal limits: no sign of infection, anemia, hypothyroidism, or low blood sugar was present. Ebstein-Barr viral titers were normal, as were screens for hepatitis and even psychological testing for depression. Other than the complaint of fatigue, this patient was textbook normal and (as discussed above) had been discharged without diagnosis from his past two doctors.

The patient was placed on the following regimen in an effort to improve his level of energy and feelings of well-being:

> Multivitamins at 4-8x RDA levels.
> Siberian ginseng liquid tincture 20 gtts 2x/day
> Vitamin C and bioflavinoids 1 gm 2x/day
> Ginkgo biloba liquid extract 20 gtts 2x/d
> Eldepryl 5mg 1x/day
> B12 IM injection 1x/week

Within two weeks the patient reported a strong increase in energy and a decreased need for sleep. In six weeks the patient reported no complaints and his dose of Eldepryl was diminished gradually to one 5mg pill every other day. The impact of Eldepryl even on the lower dose continued to be dramatically effective.

This regimen has been tried on two other individuals with symptoms similar to Chad's, however these patients experienced no significant improvement and after a trial of six weeks they were taken off all prescribed medications and released from care. We provide this information so that when you are thinking of using deprenyl you will take into consideration the individual nature of therapeutic outcome, especially when attempting to control brain chemistry, which is clearly a complex and multifaceted task.

Because the use of deprenyl for off-label indications has not been fully documented, the dosage for each patient must be experimented with so as to achieve the desired results. As with most medications, it is best to begin at a lower dosage and gradually increase the amount taken by the patient as long as there are no adverse side effects.

Subject 2

Bob was a 69-year-old male with complaints of an uncontrollable tremor and tongue thrusts, which at times was automatic and not within his ability to stop. Also he walked with an unsteady, halting gait. In addition, Bob hadn't had sexual activity in over 3 years due to impotence. Bob was already receiving Parlodel and L-Dopa for early Parkinson's symptoms but he didn't seem to be benefiting from this drug therapy.

Bob had planned to enjoy his retirement by traveling with his wife. However, because of his poor physical condition, he was embarrassed to go out of the house at all. Bob's self-esteem had plummeted so much that he no longer enjoyed spending time with his grandchildren and children.

At ALRI, Bob was placed on a high dose antioxidant vitamin formula including vitamins A, C, E, selenium,

B-complex, B1, B12, choline and the herb ginkgo biloba. Ginkgo biloba has been shown to improve cerebral circulation and may act within the brain as a central anti-oxidant. To this regimen was added Eldepryl 5mg 2x/day. In the space of months the results in Bob were startling. He had regained sexual function, his hand and tongue tremors were gone, and his gait was much improved. In addition, the slowness and hesitation of speech which he had been afflicted with for years was gone as well. It has been three years since Bob has begun therapy and if anything, his condition has continued to improve.

Subject 3

Jay, a 49-year-old entrepreneur businessman had come to the offices of ALRI with a host of non-specific complaints ranging from difficulty sleeping to low energy to just feeling burnt out. He said he felt anxious about his work and that he was having trouble concentrating. While at work he said he would often sit and stare out the window, worrying about his future. As his productivity shrank, so too, did his salary. He was beginning to lose clients and had stopped looking for new ones. To make matter worse he was also having problems with his relationship with his wife and children. His wife had threatened to leave him if he did not snap out of this "phase." His children were distant and tried to avoid all contact with him.

Jay had been through a host of treatments that had failed to benefit him including psychological counselling, psychiatric counselling as well as drug therapies that included medications given to him for his apparent depression. At ALRI, lab testing revealed nothing out of the ordinary. Yet he definitely appeared

247

to be depressed and anxious. A course of high potency vitamins and a monitored exercise program produced only limited results. So after six weeks, the patient, who after reading about deprenyl in *Longevity* magazine, asked me to prescribe it for him. He had been very impressed by its reported anti-aging properties and wanted to try it for himself, saying, "Doc, I'm starting to feel my age and I don't like it very much."

Jay was started on Eldepryl, 5mg, once a day. After two weeks with little improvement, his dose was increased to 10mg/day and improvement was noticeable almost at once. Because Jay was so anxious to find a cure for his symptoms, after three weeks he independently exceeded the maximum recommended dosage of 10mg/day by increasing the dose, on his own, and taking an additional 1/2 of a 5mg tablet daily.

Within 16 days Jay felt better than he had in 5 years. His energy returned, his sleep patterns returned to normal and the patient's productivity at work increased dramatically. While working he no longer felt depressed or anxious. Also, relations with his wife and children were greatly improved. Eventually we reduced his dose to 5mg/day and he has maintained excellent health and a happy home life at that dose for the past 2 years without any sign of a relapse.

Subject 4

LEX THE WONDER DOG

Airedales, which are a breed of Terriers, normally do not live beyond 14 years of age. Yet my pet Lex is a 13 year + rejuvenated tribute to the efficacy of antiaging medications including Deprenyl. At age 11 Lex was beginning to look like a dog of age 77 (one year in a dog's life is said to be comparable to seven years of a human's lifespan). He had difficulties walking up stairs, the spring was long gone from his gait, his eyes had become cloudy and his nose had turned from a healthy and youthful shiny black to a dried mottled grey. His his shiny coat of brown and black fur had gone grey and he hardly responded to his call.

It was clear that Lex was beginning to suffer and because I love my dog, I knew that if he did not get better soon, I would have to take drastic and permanent action. So I began Lex on a therapy consisting of two children's vitamins a day and 5 mg of Eldepryl every other day. To this I added a second exercise period of walking each day and I changed Lex's diet. One day each week Lex fasted and was allowed only water and vitamins, in order to help him lose the fat that had accumulated on his flanks.

After nine months, Lex's coat is now mostly black and brown, at least 75% of the grey has disappeared, his nose is now shiny black, his bark, which had become whiny and anemic is now full-throated, deep and commanding, and his eyes are now bright with only the slightest hint of cloudiness to his eyes. His energy level is currently up to the level of the three 6-year-old dogs in the park with whom he can now freely romp and dash about. In addition, he now has no difficulty climbing three flights of stairs, whereas before he nearly needed to be carried because his hind quarters seemed to be arthritic as seen by his unsteady and sideways gait. Lex now walks and runs straight and true and is for all appearances a normal, healthy 7-year-old Airedale capable of sexual activity, which he is now proud to show us when given the opportunity to play with female golden retrievers. It seems Lex prefers blondes.[1]

A partial list of anti-aging drugs and nutrients currently in use at the American Longevity Research Institute include the following: Eldepryl (deprenyl), DHEA (dehydroepiandroseterone), PBN Spintrap antioxidant compounds, Niacin, CoQ10, Chromium Piconate, Folic Acid, Ginkgo Biloba Extract, Panothenic Acid B-Complex, Ginseng, Hydergine, Green Tea Extract, Garlic, Malic Acid, Growth Hormone agents and releasing nutrients, and vitamins A, C, and E.

DR. RONALD KLATZ
President
American Longevity Research Institute
Chicago, IL 60614

---

[1] I chose to include the dramatic benefits of deprenyl when given my beloved Lex, not to suggest deprenyl's use for animals (even though it has been patented for that use) but rather because it is through tests on animals that we gain insights as to a drug's long-term effect on humans. If deprenyl does for humans what it did for Lex, people who are feeling the effects of their advanced years will experience a marked improvement. And, health conscious people who take deprenyl as an anti-aging/preventive "medicine", may well remain "youthful" even at a very advanced age because all tests made to-date indicate deprenyl will, in all probability, do for humans as it has for Lex.

B

Deprenyl Abstracts

Life Extension Study, Dr. Knoll

THE STRIATAL DOPAMINE DEPENDENCY OF LIFESPAN IN MALE RATS. LONGEVITY STUDY WITH (-)DEPRENYL.

JOSEPH KNOLL

Department of Pharmacology, Semmelweis University of Medicine, Budapest, P.O.B. 370, H-1445 (Hungary)

(Received September 12th, 1988)

SUMMARY

Long-term experiments on male rats revealed that better performers in the mating test are better learners in the shuttle box and the more active animals live significantly longer than their less active peers.

It was established by the aid of (-)deprenyl, a highly specific chemical tool, which increases superoxide dismutase activity in the striatum, facilitates the activity of the nigrostriatal dopaminergic neurons with utmost selectivity, and protects these neurons from their age-related decay, that the efficiency of a male rat in behavioral tests, as well as the duration of its life are striatal dopamine dependent functions.

As a measure of striatal function, sexual activity was tested once a week in a group of male rats (n=132) from the 24th month of their life. Because of the age-related decay of this function none of the 2-year-old animals displayed full-scale sexual activity. By dividing the group equally the rats were treated with saline (1 ml/kg, s.c.) and deprenyl (0.25 mg/kg, s.c.), respectively, three times a week. In the saline-treated group (n=66) the last signs of sexual activity vanished to the 33rd week of treatment. (-)Deprenyl treatment restored full-scale sexual activity in 64 out of 66 rats.

The longest living rat in the saline-treated group lived 164 weeks. The average lifespan of the group was 147.05 ± 0.56 weeks. The shortest living animal in the (-)deprenyl-treated group lived 171 weeks and the longest living rat died during the 226th week of its life. The average lifespan was 197.98 ± 2.36 weeks, i.e. higher than the estimated maximum age of death in the rat (182 weeks). This is the first instance that by the aid of a well-aimed medication members of a species lived beyond the known lifespan maximum.

Key words: Striatal dopamine; Aging of the striatum; (-)Deprenyl; Sexual activity; Learning; Superoxide dimutase activity; Rat lifespan maximum.

For Dr. Knoll's complete study see:
Mechanisms of Ageing and Development, 46 (1988) 237-262
Elsevier Scientific Publishers   Ireland Ltd.

Life Extension Study, Dr. Milgram

MAINTENACE ON L-DEPRENYL PROLONGS LIFE IN AGED MALE RATS.

NORTON W. MILGRAM[1], RONALD J. RACINE[2], PAMELA NELLIS[2], ATONIO MENDONCA[1] AND GWEN O. IVY[1]

[1]Department of Psychology, Scarborough Campus, University of Toronto, Toronto, Ont. M1C 1A4, Canada

[2]Department of Psychology, McMaster University, Hamilton, Ont. L8S 1B9 Canada

(Received in final form May 29, 1990)

SUMMARY

The effect of l-deprenyl on longevity was examined in male Fischer rats. Subcutaneous injections of either l-deprenyl (0.25 mg/kg) or saline were given every other day starting at 23 to 25 months of age. The deprenyl-treated animals showed a significant increase in both mean and maximum survival. The differences were largest in the longest surviving animals, suggesting that an earlier onset for treatment may be beneficial. Analysis of body weights ruled out deprenyl-induced dietary restriction as an explanation for the group differences in survival. To the contrary, after about four months of treatment, the animals on l-deprenyl showed a slower rate of decrease in body weight than the controls.

*To whom correspondence should be addressed:

For the complete study see:
Life Sciences, Vol. 47, pp 415–420.

Life Extension Study, Dr. Kitani

The following abstract is from an oral presentation given by Dr. Kitani at the AGE CONFERENCE, October 19, 1992, at the University of Nebraska.

CHRONIC TREATMENT OF (-)DEPRENYL PROLONGS THE LIFE SPAN OF MALE FISCHER 344 RATS.

M. C. CARRILLO[1], S. KANAI[1], Y. SATO[1], G. O. IVY[2], K. KITANI[1]

[1]Dept. of Clinical Physiology, Tokyo Metro. Inst. Gerontol. Tokyo, Japan
[2]Div. of Life Sciences, U of Toronto, Scarborough, Ontario M1C 1A4, Canada

SUMMARY

Previous two studies have shown that the chronic administration of (-)deprenyl starting from 24 months of age significantly prolonged the life span of male rats (1,2). We wanted to confirm results of these previous studies. Thirty-five male Fischer 344 (F-344) rats started to be treated with s.c. injection of (-)deprenyl (0.5 mg/kg) 3 times a week at the age of 18 months. Thirty-five control animals of the same age were treated with a physiological saline solution injection. The mean survival times after the start of treatment (18 months) and after 24 months were 378.3 ± 97.4 days (mean $\pm$ SD) and 196.3 ± 97.4 days respectively in deprenyl treated rats and both 328.7 days, 146.7 + 108.7 days in control rats. Increases in average life expectancies (15% from 18 months and 34% from 24 months) caused by deprenyl treatment were both statistically significant (P 0.05, two-tailed t-test). The average body weights were comparable for both groups excluding the possibility that the effect of deprenyl is secondary from the reduced diet intake caused by this treatment. The results confirm the previous two studies (1,2) which reported a significant life prolonging effect of this drug in aged rats and support more strongly the result of a study on male F-344 rats where the effect was only marginally significant (16% increase after 24 months, P=0.048 by one-tailed t-test) (2). Ref. 1. Mech Ageing Dev 46:237, 1988. 2. Life Sci. 47:415, 1990.

Effect on SOD and Catalase, Dr. Kitani

The following abstract is from an oral presentation given by Dr. Kitani at the AGE CONFERENCE, October 19, 1992, at the University of Nebraska.

SEQUENTIAL CHANGES IN ACTIVITIES OF SUPEROXIDE DISMUTASE (SOD) AND CATALASE (CAT) IN BRAIN REGIONS AND LIVER DURING (-)DEPRENYL INFUSION IN MALE RATS.

M. C. CARRILLO[1], S. KANAI[1], Y. SATO[1], G. O. IVY[2], K. KITANI[1]

[1]Dept. of Clinical Physiology, Tokyo Metro. Inst. Gerontol. Tokyo, Japan
[2]Div. of Life Sciences, U of Toronto, Scarborough, Ontario M1C 1A4, Canada

SUMMARY

Previous studies including those of our own have shown that (-)deprenyl causes increases in SOD and CAT activities in striatum in rats. Our own study further has shown that this effect is selective for certain brain regions. Thus far all studies adhered to the duration of deprenyl administration for 3 weeks. The present study aimed to clarify sequential changes in these enzyme activities during deprenyl treatment. A continuous S.C. infusion of (-)deprenyl in young male rats at a dose of 2.0 mg/kg/day for 1 week significantly increased SOD activities (both Cu Zn-SOD and Mn-SOD) in certain brain regions such as substantia nigra and striatum but not in hippocampus or cerebellum or in the liver. With continuing infusion, SOD activities were further increased in the following weeks, reaching a plateau at 3 weeks. In cerebral cortices the increase became significant at 3 weeks. In contrast, an increase in CAT activity became significant only after 2 weeks of infusion, and only in the same brain regions where SOD activities were increased earlier. The delay in the increase of CAT activity following deprenyl infusion suggests a possibility that this is an adaptive response to the earlier increase in deprenyl-induced SOD activities rather than a direct effect of deprenyl on CAT, although the latter possibility cannot be excluded.

Rescue of Dying Neurons, Dr. Tatton

Journal of Neuroscience Research, 30:666-672 (1991)

RESCUE OF DYING NEURONS: A NEW ACTION FOR DEPRENYL IN MPTP PARKINSONISM.

W. G. TATTON AND C. E. GREENWOOD

Centre for Research on Neurodegenerative Disorders, Departments of Physiology and Psychiatry (W.G.T.): and Nutritional Sciences (C.E.G.), Faculty of Medicine, University of Toronto, Toronto, Ontario M5S 1A8, Canada.

ABSTRACT

Deprenyl slows the progression of disabling symptoms in Parkinson's disease (PD) by an unknown mechanism. It can block the action of MPTP on substantia nigra compacta (SNc) neurons by inhibiting monoamine oxidase B necessary to mediate the conversion of MPTP to MPP+, its active metabolite, in astroglia. Mice were pretreated with saline or the PD-producing toxin, MPTP (30 mg/kg) daily for 5 days and then after a further 3 days (to allow for the metabolism and excretion of the MPTP) were treated with deprenyl (0.25 or 10 mg/kg) or saline 3 times weekly for 20 days. In three series of mice treated with MPTP alone or MPTP-saline, serial sections through the SNc showed that averages of 37-12% of tyrosine hydroxylase (TH) immunoreactive neurons were lost gradually over 20 days. Joint counts of the numbers of TH-immunoreactive and Nissl-stained SNc somata from immediately adjacent sections established that the reductions in the numbers of TH-immunoreactive somata at 20 days after MPTP treatment represented neuronal death. Deprenyl treatment reduced the loss of TH-immunoreactive SNc neurons to averages of 14-16% for the 10-mg/kg and 0.25-mg/kg doses, respectively, and joint Nissl/TH counts for adjacent sections showed that reducton in the loss of TH-immunoreactive soma represented the rescue of SNc neurons that would have died by 20 days. The gradual loss of SNc neurons over the 20 days following MPTP exposure may reflect the toxin's axotomy-like effects on SNc neurons or the prolonged action of sequestered MPP+. In either case, the research shows that deprenyl can increase SNc neuronal survival by a mechanism that is independent of the blockade of MPTP's conversion to MPP+ and may be responsible for slowing the progression of PD.

Address reprint requests to:
Dr. William G. Tatton, Center for Research in Neurodegenerative Diseases, Tanz Neuroscience Building, 6 Queens Park Crescent West, Toronto, Ontario M5S 1A8, Canada.

C

ABOUT THE AUTHOR
AND CONTRIBUTORS

Alastair Dow

When Dr. Morton Shulman asked himself who was
the best investigative reporter/author to tell the story
of deprenyl, his immediate choice was Alastair Dow,
one of the few authors, ever, to win Canada's presti-
gious National Business Award — three times.

Intrigued by the story of deprenyl and Dr. Shulman's much-improved physical condition since taking
deprenyl, Alastair Dow traveled to Budapest, Vienna,
and London, as well as cities throughout Canada and
the United States to learn, first hand, the story of deprenyl and its amazing life extension benefits.

Alastair Dow works independently as a researcher
and writer. Mr. Dow is married, has three sons and
lives in Toronto, Canada.

Dr. Ronald M. Klatz

Dr. Klatz is recognized as one of the world's authorities in preventive/longevity medicine and maximum

human performance. He has published extensively and was co-author of the best selling books *Death in the Locker Room/Steroids & Sports*, and *The E Factor*. Dr. Klatz has been a syndicated columnist for Pioneer Press of Chicago, a division of Time-Life Inc., hosted his own radio show, and served as an advisor to Physicians Radio Network. He is also senior medical editor for *Longevity Magazine.*

Dr. Klatz is Board Certified by the American Osteopathic Board of General Practice, American Osteopathic Academy of Sports Medicine, and the Academy of Sports Physicians.

American Longevity Research Institute, a not for profit research foundation exploring new life extension technologies, was founded by Dr. Klatz who is also president of Life Technologies, Inc., a medical invention company recently awarded a patent on a brain resuscitation device.

Dr. Klatz is co-founder of the National Academy of Sports Medicine, co-publisher of the *Professional's Journal of Sports Fitness; The NASM Journal of Certified Personal Fitness Trainers* and *Health-Care USA*, news magazine.

Saul Kent

Saul Kent is one of the foremost life extension activists in the United States. He is President of The Life Extension Foundation, a non-profit organization dedicated to the dissemination of accurate information about the latest world-wide life extension research and therapies. Kent has written books on the subject, including *The Life Extension Revolution* (Wm. Morrow, 1980) and *Your Personal Life Extension Program* (Wm. Morrow, 1985) as well as numerous articles for medical and lay publications. He also has conducted conferences and seminars to help people live longer in good health, and appears frequently on radio and TV programs to discuss issues related to life extension.

D

PUBLISHER'S NOTE

WHEN THE OPPORTUNITY to publish this book presented itself, I seized it immediately because I knew from personal experience that deprenyl is truly a miracle drug; one that can, not only help those with various neurological diseases, but one that can help prevent them — and — allow you and I to remain vigorous and "youthful" in our later years.

Product Name

Deprenyl tablets are sold in the United States under the trade name Eldepryl. The active ingredient in deprenyl products is selegiline.

Selegiline was developed in 1960 by Chinoin Pharmaceutical and Chemical Works, Ltd., of Budapest, Hungary. Deprenyl is its official name in all scientific literature because this is the name Chinoin registered with the *World Health Organization*.

Deprenyl began being called "Eldepryl" in English

speaking countries after success in treating Parkinson's Disease and other neurological conditions was discovered.

Product Information

The active ingredient in any "deprenyl" product is *selegiline*. There are a number of companies offering high quality selegiline. For information on domestic and foreign sources of deprenyl *tablets* write or phone the Life Extension Foundation, P.O. Box 229120, Hollywood, FL 33022.

For information on deprenyl *liquid*, phone Discovery Pharmaceutical Company, (813) 973-7354 and ask for Dept. 1053. Their mailing address is Discovery Pharmaceutical Company, Dept. 1053, 29949 S.R. 54 West, Wesley Chapel, FL 33543.

Availability For Anti-Aging Purposes

In spite of an unblemished safety record, you have to obtain a prescription to buy Eldepryl in the United States. We hope more doctors will read this book and be willing to prescribe Eldepryl for general anti-aging purposes. Doctors are allowed to prescribe Eldepryl to treat diseases other than Parkinson's, and as more and more doctors become informed about Eldepryl's ability to prevent and treat a variety of diseases, we expect it will be easier to find a cooperative doctor. Why not make your doctor a gift of this book. I am certain that once he has had a chance to review it, you will find the doctor very willing to prescribe Eldepryl on your next visit. Should you be searching for a doctor that practices "preventive" medicine, the Life Extension Foundation has compiled a nation-wide directory of Life Extension Doctors who are knowledge-

able about prescribing Eldepryl for anti-aging purposes. You can obtain a free copy of this directory by
calling 1-800-841-5433.

Last but not least, if you have a question concerning
a given drug, phone Dr. Alan Zimmer at the Mail
Order Pharmacy, 1-800-822-5388. Dr. Zimmer is a foremost authority, researcher and writer on pharmaceuticals who is currently writing a wide-ranging textbook on pharmaceutical drug developments worldwide for use in graduate schools of pharmacology.

I close with the wish that this book may help you
enjoy life to the fullest.

CHARLES HALLBERG
Publisher